Simon Seivewright

RESEARCH AND DESIGN

n. The systematic investigation into and
study of materials and sources

n. A drawing produced to show the look
and function or workings of a garment
before it is made

An AVA Book

Published by AVA Publishing SA

Rue des Fontenailles 16, Case Postale, 1000 Lausanne 6, Switzerland

Tel: +41 786 005 109

Email: enquiries@avabooks.ch

Distributed by Thames & Hudson (ex-North America)

181a High Holborn, London WC1V 7QX, United Kingdom

Tel: +44 20 7845 5000

Fax: +44 20 7845 5055

Email: sales@thameshudson.co.uk

www.thamesandhudson.com

Distributed in the USA & Canada by:

Watson-Guptill Publications, 770 Broadway, New York, New York 10003, USA

Fax: +1 646 654 5487

Email: info@watsonguptill.com

www.watsonguptill.com

English Language Support Office

AVA Publishing (UK) Ltd.

Tel: +44 1903 204 455

Email: enquiries@avabooks.co.uk

ISBN 2-940373-41-8 and 978-2-940373-41-3

10 9 8 7 6 5 4 3 2 1

Design by Sifer Design

Original book and series concept devised by Natalia Price-Cabrera

Production by AVA Book Production Pte. Ltd., Singapore

Tel: +65 6334 8173

Fax: +65 6259 9830

Email: production@avabooks.com.sg

'Fashion is very important. It is life-enhancing and, like everything that gives pleasure, it is worth doing well.'

Vivienne Westwood

<u>1</u>
Silk evening top and skirt;
Christian Dior; 1953. V&A
Images/Victoria and Albert
Museum.

Contents

Research and Design

Contents

1
Christian Dior haute couture
S/S07. Designer John Galliano.

'Creative research is the secret or trick which underlines all original design.'

John Galliano, creative director, Dior

Research is vital to any design process; it is the initial trawl and collection of ideas prior to design. It should be an experimental process, an investigation to support or find out about a particular subject. Research is an essential tool in the creative process and will provide inspiration, information and creative direction, as well as a narrative to a collection. Research is about a journey that can often take weeks or even months to collate and process. It is also a very personal activity, which through its manifestation, provides the viewer with an insight into the thinking, aspirations, interests and creative vision of the designer.

From in-depth and broad-ranging research, the designer can begin to interpret a series of garments or a collection. Silhouettes, textures, colours, details, print and embellishment will all have their place in the process of design and will all be found in the research created.

BASICS Fashion Design: Research and Design will lead you through the essential stages of research and translation into design ideas. It will discuss elements such as the brief and the constraints it can place on the research and design process. It will explain the importance of identifying your target market and understanding the different levels and genres of fashion before setting out on the creative research. It will then discuss the many avenues for researching and the need to set a theme, concept or narrative to your collection. The book then explains how you translate your research into early design ideas and techniques used in bridging the gap between research and design. Design development is also explained and communicated through a series of structured stages. Finally the book shows and explores a variety of approaches to communicating and rendering your design work.

Research and Design will provide you with the fundamental skills and knowledge to start you on the journey of designing an in-depth, innovative and creative collection. Good luck and enjoy the creative process.

Introduction

How to get the most out of this book

This book introduces different aspects of fashion research and design via dedicated chapters for each topic. Each chapter provides numerous examples of work by leading fashion designers, annotated to explain the reasons behind choices made.

Key fashion research and design principles are isolated so that the reader can see how they are applied in practice.

Clear navigation
Each chapter has a clear strapline to allow readers to quickly locate areas of interest.

Quotes
Key points are elaborated on and placed in context through the use of quotes.

What is research?

1
Selection of research material gathered; from wallpaper designs to buttons, trims to sketchbook references.

'The systematic investigation into the study of materials and sources in order to establish facts and reach new conclusions.'

Oxford Dictionary of English

Fashion by its very definition is about current popular custom or style; the fashion designer expresses the zeitgeist, or spirit of the times in their work. Fashion is constantly changing and the designer is expected to recreate the wheel every season. Because of this constant pressure for the new, designers have to dig ever deeper and search ever further for new inspiration and ways of interpreting this into their collections. Fashion designers are therefore like magpies, obsessive collectors, and always on the hunt for new and exciting things to inspire them. The need to gather and source material for use in the creative process is essential for feeding the imagination.

Research is about investigation, learning about something new or from the past. It can often be likened to the beginning of a journey of exploration. It is about reading, visiting or perhaps viewing, but above all, it is about recording information.

There are two types of research. The first is gathering the tangible and practical materials for your collection – for example, fabric, trims, buttons. The other is about the visual inspiration for the collection, and this will often help to set the theme, mood or concept that is essential in developing an identity for your creative work. Research should be broad ranging and in-depth, enabling you to innovate, not imitate in the collection you create from it.

Research could be likened to a diary or journal, a snapshot of who you are, what you are interested in and what is happening in the world at a specific time. Trends, social and political issues could be documented and all have impact on the research and creative design process. This information, diary, research, is something that could be used in the present, now, or in the future.

'Research is formalized curiosity. It is poking and prying with a purpose.'

Zora Neale Hurston
American folklorist and writer, 1891–1960

Introductions
Special section introductions outline basic concepts that will be discussed.

Examples
Projects from contemporary designers bring the principles under discussion alive.

Research and Design

Headings
Enabling the reader to break down text and refer quickly to topics of interest.

Additional information
Box-outs elaborate on subjects discussed in the main text.

Captions
Provide image details and commentary to guide the reader in the exploration of the visuals displayed.

Magazines

Knowing your subject and having an awareness of fashion is an essential part of the research process and magazines are a good place to develop this knowledge.

Magazines are a great source of information and potential inspiration for the designer; they can firstly provide you with images of the latest trends, styles and garments from other designers in the industry, and secondly give you insight into other aspects you should consider as a designer, for example, lifestyle and cultural interests that may affect the market you wish to design for.

Looking at other designers' collections is not so that you can copy what they are doing, but to give you an understanding of what has already been created and the possibilities that are open to you. There are so many different magazines out on the news-stands these days that you should not simply gravitate towards the obvious ones, such as Vogue and Elle. There are many more fashion, art and lifestyle publications that focus on niche markets that you should be aware of. These magazines are filled with new up-and-coming talent and feature not just on the clothes' designers, but also on the art direction, hair and make-up artists, photographers and stylists.

Building your knowledge of designers, trends and lifestyle habits is not something that will happen overnight and should be something that is done regularly over time so that it will help you establish yourself within the industry.

As a student you may well be asked to recall your favourite designers or the publications you read by your tutors as a way of demonstrating your knowledge and interest in the subject. But equally you may be asked to begin market research by using magazines for a design team in a large high street company, so it is important to understand this part of the process at an early stage in your career.

Magazines to investigate: *International Textiles, View, Uomo Book, Wonderland, Fashion, Vogue, In Fashion, Bloom, Another Magazine, View 2, 10.*

1
Knowing your subject: here is a selection of magazine titles you should be aware of.

Chapter titles
Run up the side of every page to provide clear navigation and allow the reader to understand the context of the information on the page.

Running footers
Clear navigation allows the reader to know where they are, where they have come from and where they are going.

How to get the most out of this book

Example of a research-inspired collaged figure.

'Research is what I'm doing when I don't know what I'm doing.'

Wernher von Braun

Research is about creative investigation, it is about recording information for use now or in the future. But what exactly is it? Designers are constantly looking for new ideas, fashion by its very nature is always changing and reinventing itself, but where does it all start?

In this first chapter we aim to demystify what research is, as well as explore the creative investigation process. It also looks at why you should research in the first place. The chapter discusses what a brief is, the different types of brief and what it is the designer is being asked to do. What do you need to consider as a designer before you start any project or collection? This is a question every designer should ask himself or herself. The chapter then goes on to explain what the purpose of research is and what it should contain in terms of information.

Above all, the process of research should be fun, exciting, informative and most importantly useful.

What is a brief?

1

Julien Macdonald's design illustration for the new British Airways' uniform.
Courtesy of NewsCast.

The brief is usually the start to any creative project and the project is a sustained body of work that is normally time bound. The purpose of a brief is essentially to inspire you and outline the aims and objectives that are required. It will identify any constraints, conditions or problems that need to be solved, as well as providing you with information on what final outcomes or tasks are to be achieved. The brief is there to help you and more importantly to guide the whole research and design process.

British Airways brief, as discussed with Julien Macdonald:

What was the brief British Airways set you as a designer?

I was asked along with many other designers to come up with a set of sketches for uniforms that could be worn by all the different British Airways staff from all over the world. The uniforms had to be functional pieces that could be worn by the cabin crew to the ground staff to the baggage handlers, over 80,000 employees worldwide.

The designs were submitted anonymously to the British Airways board of directors and design team so that the ideas would not be judged on the name of the designer. They were really surprised when they found out that the clean, simple stylish ideas were mine, as they associated my name with glitz and glamour!

What were the constraints you had?

There were many complex constraints as the investment by the company was worth millions of pounds and the last time it was changed was over ten years ago, when Paul Costelloe did the designs.

The clothes had to fit from a size 6 to 22, both men and women, and there was to be no discrimination between race, colour or creed. The garments had to be in the same fabric, whether you were working in a Russian winter or the summer in the Seychelles. I spent time working alongside the staff to find out about their working lives from leaving their homes to go to work to then arriving in a hotel after a ten-hour flight and having to wash the blouse in the sink to have it fresh for the return flight the next morning!

The garments where given a pilot period where we looked at how they performed under the normal working conditions. For example, did the fabric wear well? Did the buttons fall off etc.? The final garments were then successfully put into production and can be seen on any current flight with British Airways.

1

Types of brief

There are several types of brief. The most common one is found within the academic forum where it is usually set by the tutor and asks you as an individual to respond to it. The aims are what you are expected to learn and the objectives will be the work demonstrated. As the student you will be expected to answer not only the brief's creative requirements, but also the assessment criteria that will be clearly identified. The brief is used as an important tool by the tutor to help teach specific skills and develop and improve your knowledge and understanding.

Another type of brief also found within the academic forum is one for a competition often set by a company or external organisation as a way of promoting products or a brand and in turn, encouraging new talent within the industry. This association with industry will often provide sponsorship, placement awards and travel bursaries for the students taking part.

Commercial and client based are the other types of briefs you will come across as a designer. These will have very specific aims and objectives that will consider some or all of the following: market, season, genres, cost and occasion. The true measure of your creativity as a designer will be to achieve something exciting and innovative while considering very closely what you are being asked to produce and adhering to the constraints of the brief in order to achieve the client's approval.

A good example of a designer working to a specific commercial brief would be Julien Macdonald, who redesigned British Airways' employees' uniform. Here the brief would have had very specific criteria and restrictions on design, use of fabric, cost, function and performance.

Another common type of brief is one that asks you to work within a team, for example, a large high street brand. Here you will be expected to work with others on a project and you will have specific tasks assigned to you that will ultimately work towards presenting a coherent and cohesive collection.

Occasion and season: As a designer it is important to be aware of when you are designing for, as it will have an impact on many of the design factors, such as fabric and colour.

Muse or customer: A brief will sometimes ask you to design for a very specific consumer of a certain age, size and gender. It may also ask you to build a customer profile and consider elements such as background, work, lifestyle and income.

Target market: A brief will often ask you to focus on a specific market sector in the industry, such as high street or middle-market price points. This again requires you to consider market analysis and customer profiling.

Material and fabric: Sometimes in the academic field you will be asked to problem solve a brief that focuses your creativity on the use of a particular type or quality of fabric; for example, jersey.

Costing: Most project briefs, whether they are academic or industry set, will require you to consider the price that something will cost.

Practical outcomes: This is simply what you are expected to produce. The brief may have a specific garment type as its final outcome, for example, a dress, a jacket, or a piece of knitwear.

What is research?

1

Selection of research material gathered; from wallpaper designs to buttons, trims to sketchbook references.

'The systematic investigation into the study of materials and sources in order to establish facts and reach new conclusions.'

Oxford Dictionary of English

Fashion by its very definition is about current popular custom or style; the fashion designer expresses the zeitgeist, or spirit of the times in their work. Fashion is constantly changing and the designer is expected to recreate the wheel every season. Because of this constant pressure for the new, designers have to dig ever deeper and search ever further for new inspiration and ways of interpreting this into their collections. Fashion designers are therefore like magpies, obsessive collectors, and always on the hunt for new and exciting things to inspire them. The need to gather and source material for use in the creative process is essential for feeding the imagination.

Research is about investigation, learning about something new or from the past. It can often be likened to the beginning of a journey of exploration. It is about reading, visiting or perhaps viewing, but above all, it is about recording information.

There are two types of research. The first is gathering the tangible and practical materials for your collection – for example, fabric, trims, buttons. The other is about the visual inspiration for the collection, and this will often help to set the theme, mood or concept that is essential in developing an identity for your creative work. Research should be broad ranging and in-depth, enabling you to innovate, not imitate in the collection you create from it.

Research could be likened to a diary or journal, a snapshot of who you are, what you are interested in and what is happening in the world at a specific time. Trends, social and political issues could be documented and all have impact on the research and creative design process. This information, diary, research, is something that could be used in the present, now, or in the future.

'Research is formalized curiosity. It is poking and prying with a purpose.'

Zora Neale Hurston
American folklorist and writer, 1891–1960

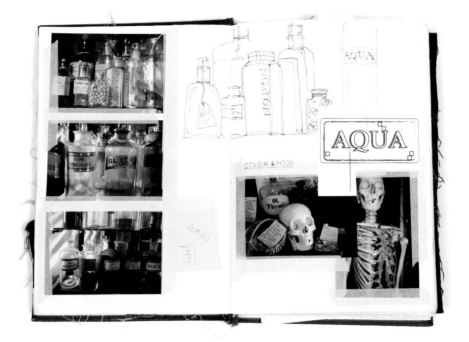

1

2

What is its purpose?

We know what research is, but why do we need it? How does it help you as a designer?

Research is there, above all, to inspire you as a creative individual. It is a way of stimulating the mind and opening up new directions in design. By gathering different references and exploring many avenues of interest you can begin to explore a variety of creative possibilities before you channel and focus your imagination towards a concept, theme or direction for a collection.

Research will help you learn about a subject. You might discover information previously unknown to you, or perhaps new skills or technologies could be explored.

Research is an opportunity to inquire into your own interests and expand your awareness and knowledge of the world around you. As a result, research is very much a personal and individual task, and although a team of people can gather it, one person generally has the creative vision and takes the lead.

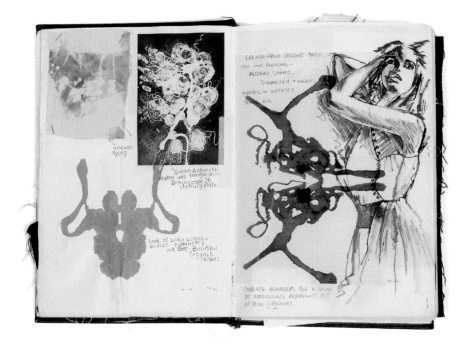

uneven
dying

Susan Aldworth
Matter into Imagination
Brainscape 26
etching Plate

Look at brain scans—
bodies symmetry
ink Blots— Beautiful
organic
shapes

CREATE PRINT DESIGNS BASED
ON INK BLOTCHES.
ABSTRACT SHAPES,
SYMMETRY + MIRROR
IMAGES → DISTORTED
ETC.

OVER-USE ROUGHEDGES FOR A SENSE
OF MERICULOUS RESTRAINT. PUT
IN FREE DRAWINGS.

3

Research is a way of showing the world how you see it and how you think. And this is extremely important in differentiating you from everyone else in the industry. Think of it as a personal diary of a moment in your creative lifetime and a document to show whoever is interested what has inspired you and had an effect on your life.

The final thing to remember is that research must be above all else inspiring and useful.

1–3
Student research sketchbooks.

What should research contain?

Reichstag Building, Germany. Photograph by Nigel Young. The internal structure shown in this image links closely with that of a 19th-century crinoline. Courtesy of Nigel Young/Foster + Partners.

2

Historical examples of 19th-century crinolines and corsets used to exaggerate the human silhouette. Dover Press.

3

Example of a student sketchbook clearly demonstrating the influence of architecture on garment design.

As already discussed, research is about the investigation and recording of information. This information is something that can be broken down into a series of categories that will help to inspire you, as well as providing the different components of a collection's direction.

Shapes and structures

By its very definition, 'shape' is an area or form with a definite outline and a visible appearance and structure. It is also the way in which something is constructed or supported in a framework. Shapes are a vital element of research and ultimately design, as they provide you with potential ideas to translate on to the body and into garments. Without shape there would be no silhouettes in fashion design.

To support shape it is also important to consider structure and how something is constructed or created. The potential to understand how a framework or parts can support shape is vital and again this can be translated into fashion design. Consider a domed roof of a cathedral or contemporary glasshouse and the crinoline frame of a 19th-century dress.

Crinoline: This is a lightweight frame constructed by connecting horizontal hoops of wire and cotton tape together. Crinolines were worn under skirts to allow the silhouette of the body to be exaggerated. Their use was at its most popular and extreme in shape during the mid to late 1800s.

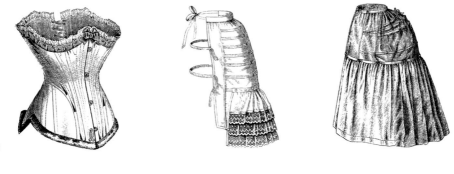

2

3

Details

As a designer it is important that you not only consider inspiration for shape in your research, but also the more practical elements like the details. The details of a garment can be anything from where the topstitching is placed to pocket types, fastenings, and shapes of cuffs and collars. The details of a garment are equally important to design as the silhouette, as these will often be the selling feature once it is given closer examination by buyers. It is therefore essential that you incorporate detailing in order to create a successful and more evolved garment.

The research gathered for this element of the design process can come from many different sources. It may be that you explore the pockets and cuffs of a military jacket or take elements from an historical garment. It may be that the details come from a more abstract source, for example, a pocket shape inspired by something more organic. The inspiration for the detailing on a garment or a whole collection should filter through from all the different sources you have researched. The detailing may not be immediately obvious, but as you will learn, it is an important part of the design process and must ultimately be considered.

1

2

Topstitching: This is any stitching visible on the right side of a garment. It can be decorative, but its main function is to reinforce a seam. It can commonly be seen in denim garments such as jeans.

<u>1</u>

Sheepskin collar detail on men's DSquared flight jacket.

<u>2</u>

Swarovski crystal button selection card.

<u>3</u>

Cuff detail on Irish Guards' military dress jacket.

<u>4</u>

Irish Guards' military dress jacket.

3

4

What is its purpose? > **What should research contain?** > Brainstorming

Colour

Colour is a fundamental consideration in the research and design process. It is often the first element that is noticed about a design and influences how that garment or collection is perceived. Colour has fascinated us since ancient times and in our clothing it reflects personality, character and taste, and can also convey significant messages reflecting different cultures and social status.

As a designer colour is often the starting point of a collection and can control the mood and season that you are designing for. The research you gather for colour should be both primary and secondary, and allow you to mix and play with a variety of combinations.

Where your inspiration comes from is limitless as we live in a world surrounded by colour. Nature, for instance, provides you with an unlimited array of colours, shades and tones that can be translated into a palette for the design process. However, your inspiration could equally come from an artist or a specific painting or period in history.

Palette: This is a piece of board that an artist mixes up paint on before painting, but as a designer it means a group of colours that are mixed together. They can coordinate, have similar hues and tones or can be juxtaposed and clash.

In chapter five we will discuss colour theory and the use of colour palettes in the design of a collection.

1

A selection of colour-themed inspiration boards.

1

Textures

Texture refers to the surface quality of objects and appeals to our sense of touch. Light and dark patterns of different textures can provide visual stimulation for the viewer without actually having to touch the object, as well as describing the surface that is presented.

As a fashion designer, research into texture will ultimately lead to fabric and the many different qualities and finishes available to you. The way something looks and feels on the body is a crucial part of the design process, but inspiration for this can come from many different sources.

The textures you research can often inspire new ideas for surface manipulation and the way a fabric handles will help to define and possibly shape a garment. Images of building materials, landscapes and organic forms may help inspire knitwear and fabric manipulation techniques such as pleating.

1
Sophia Kokosalaki S/S06 dress
inspired by shell-like textures and
patterns. Catwalking.com.

2
Ernst Haeckel, art forms in
nature, drawings of seashells.
Dover Press.

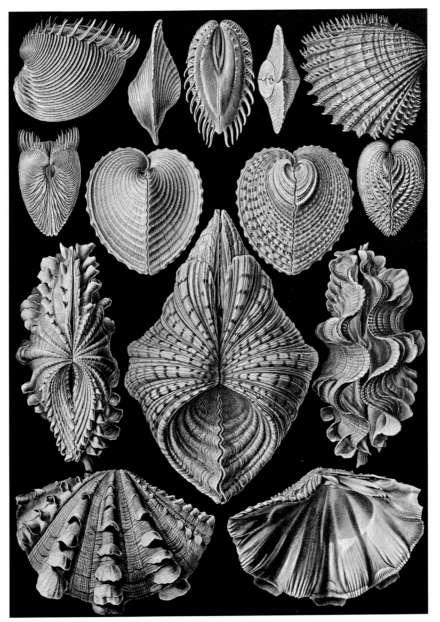

2

Research: what and why?

Print and surface decoration

Through the process of research you may well start to gather information and references that have natural patterns or decorations on them and lend themselves to be interpreted into print and textile development. Images or objects may well be decorative, jewelled, repeated, mirrored or provide an opportunity for a motif within a design concept.

Surface qualities may also suggest translation into textile techniques, such as embroidery, smocking, appliqué and beading. Surface finishes can be applied to a fabric or garment to alter the look, feel and perhaps reflect the mood of the source of inspiration; for example, distressed, aged and faded translated from scorched arid land in Africa. Or jewelled and decorative qualities translated from sourced Indian sari fabrics.

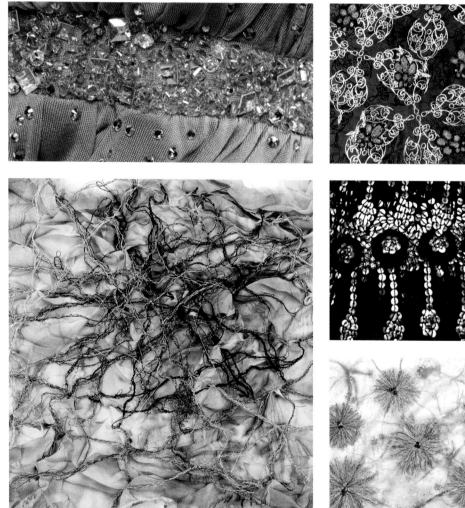

1

<u>1</u>
Details showing embroidery, beading, smocking, stitch work and appliqué.

<u>2</u>
Research board inspired by African decorative costume.

Embroidery: This is the craft of sewing thread on to the surface of a fabric to create patterns and texture. By using different types of thread and stitch you are able to create elaborate surface decoration on flat fabrics.

Smocking: This is a technique using stitch to gather fabric in a honeycomb pattern. There are many variations to this basic stitch and it allows the designer to create shape and volume in a garment without the need to cut the fabric.

Appliqué: This is a technique where a piece of cut-out fabric is sewn or fixed ornamentally to another fabric so as to create a surface decoration or pattern.

Beading: This is exactly as it sounds, the decoration of fabric with beads, usually sewn.

2

Historical influences

As with any creative field it is essential to have an understanding of what has taken place in the past so that you can move ideas and technologies forward. Historical influences may be found in any design discipline from any culture. They could be as diverse as looking at ancient tiles from an Islamic mosque to Japanese samurai armour.

A key element of historical research must be that of dress history or costume. Learning about dress history is an extremely important part of being a fashion designer and for many it has provided a treasure trove and wealth of information on everything from shape and tailoring, to fabric and embellishments. Vivienne Westwood describes the process of looking at historical dress for inspiration as 'synthesising the old into the new'. She is certainly famous for exploring many different centuries of costume to invigorate her collections.

Fashion by its definition is about current popular trends and so looking at costume provides you with an insight into trends of that period.

1

2

tacky fashion of

'It was interesting to explore historical clothes and to think about those textures, those embroideries, those materials and then to interpret them for a woman today, not as costume, but as wardrobe.'

Nicolas Ghesquiere at Balenciaga

<u>1</u>
Givenchy haute couture A/W98. Designed by Alexander McQueen, inspired by 18th-century Vandyke collars. Catwalking.com.

<u>2</u>
Christian Lacroix research sketchbook showing historical inspiration. *Christian Lacroix: The Diary of a Collection*, pp38–39. Courtesy of Thames & Hudson.

DIRECTOIR

usic program, the same lightness and DARING style

What is its purpose? > **What should research contain?** > Brainstorming

Cultural influences

Cultural influences can be everything from the appreciation of literature, arts and music from your own country to the appreciation of the customs and civilization of another. Looking at another country for ideas can provide you with a wealth of inspiration that may translate itself into colour, fabric, and print and garment shapes. Designers such as John Galliano and Jean Paul Gaultier are well known for the way they look to many different cultures as a springboard for their collections.

As a designer you may also be inspired by literature and employ this to give narrative to your collection. Current art exhibitions can have an influence on the research you gather and the creations you design. For example, a retrospective of Frida Kahlo's paintings, the Mexican painter who had a strong traditional dress style, was then clearly seen in collections by Lacroix and Gaultier.

1
Christian Dior haute couture S/S07. Designed by John Galliano, inspired by Japanese costume. Catwalking.com.

2
17th-century Japanese colour print by the artist Suzuki Harunobu. Art Media/Heritage-Images.

3–4
Jean Paul Gaultier S/S98 and A/W05, Frida Kahlo-inspired and Mexican-inspired collections. Catwalking.com.

1

2

3

Contemporary trends

Having an awareness of events and cultural trends is something you must develop as a designer. Observing global changes, social trends and political climates is essential in creating clothes for a specific target market. Tracking trends is not necessarily a fully conscious activity, but merely an ability to tune in to the spirit of the times or zeitgeist. It is also the awareness of subtle changes in taste and interests that often start out on the 'street'.

The 'bubble-up effect' describes how activities, special interests and subculture groups – often through music and exposure on television – have an influence on the mainstream and are seen as a new direction for fashion and media.

Fashion forecasting agencies and trend magazines are just some of the ways in which you can easily gain access to this sort of information.

1

1
View 2, a colour, textile and forecasting magazine.

2
In Fashion biannual fashion designer collections magazine.

Brainstorming

1

An example of a mind-map exploring the colour red and connotations thereof.

Brainstorming, or creating mind-maps, is a useful technique to explore in the initial stages of research and can help to generate many ideas that you as the designer can then delve into more deeply. Brainstorming requires you to simply list every word you can think of that relates to your project brief.

Use dictionaries, a thesaurus and the Internet to assist in this activity. Pictures can also be assigned to the words written down and therefore provide you with potential starting points for your collection and also possible ideas for a theme or concept.

Be open-minded and allow your imagination to wander into many different related and unrelated areas; the juxtaposition of words and themes can often present new concepts and marriages for the design.

1

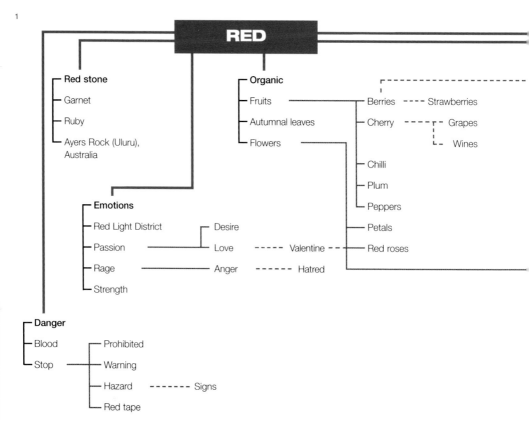

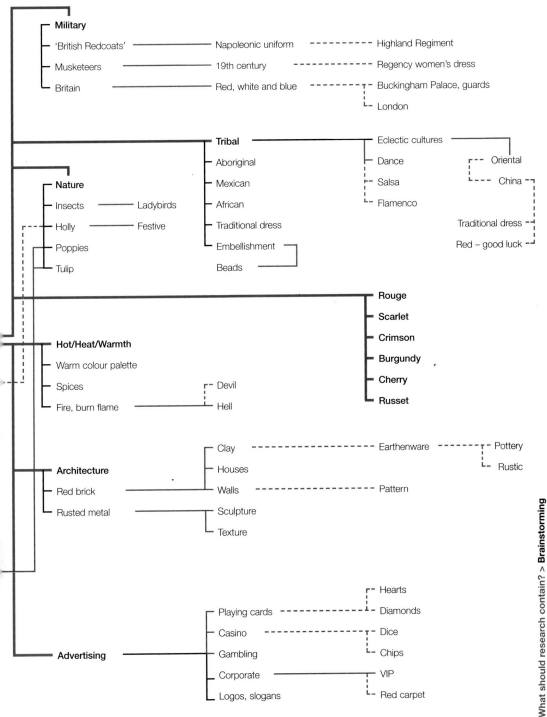

Military
- 'British Redcoats' ——————— Napoleonic uniform - - - - - - - Highland Regiment
- Musketeers ——————— 19th century - - - - - - - Regency women's dress
- Britain ——————— Red, white and blue - - - - - - - Buckingham Palace, guards
                                                                    └─ London

Tribal ——————— Eclectic cultures
- Aboriginal ├─ Dance - - - - - Oriental
- Mexican ├─ Salsa └─ China
- African └─ Flamenco
- Traditional dress   Traditional dress
- Embellishment   Red – good luck

Nature
- Insects ——— Ladybirds
- Holly ——— Festive
- Poppies
- Tulip

Beads

Rouge

Scarlet

Crimson

Burgundy

Cherry

Russet

Hot/Heat/Warmth
- Warm colour palette
- Spices ┌─ Devil
- Fire, burn flame └─ Hell

Architecture
- Red brick
- Rusted metal

- Clay - - - - - - - - Earthenware - - - - - ┌─ Pottery
- Houses   └─ Rustic
- Walls - - - - - - - - Pattern
- Sculpture
- Texture

Advertising ———
- Playing cards - - - - - - ┌─ Hearts
- Casino - - - - - - └─ Diamonds
- Gambling ┌─ Dice
- Corporate ——— VIP └─ Chips
- Logos, slogans └─ Red carpet

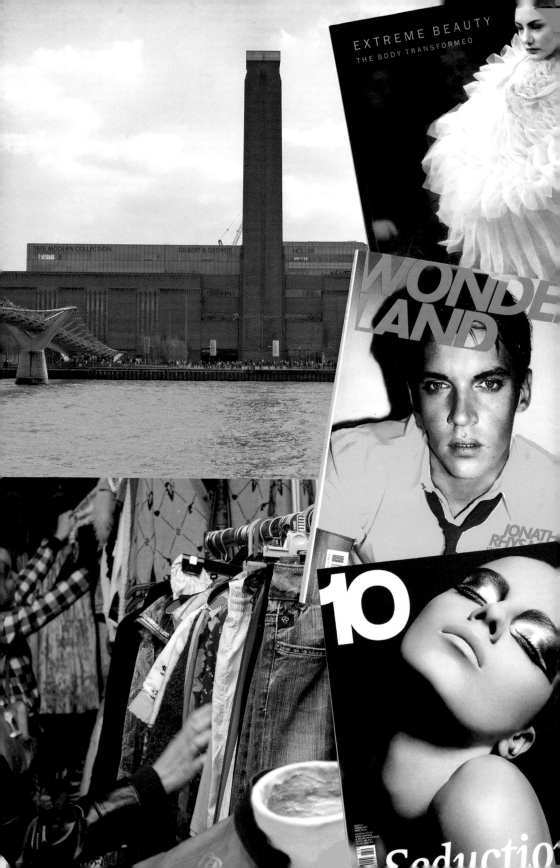

EXTREME BEAUTY
THE BODY TRANSFORMED

WONDER LAND

JONATH
RHYS

TATE MODERN COLLECTION
GILBERT & GEORGE
HÖLLER

10

Seductio

'Fashion is not something that exists in dresses only. Fashion is in the sky, in the street, fashion has to do with ideas, the way we live, what is happening.'

Coco Chanel, 1883–1971

Inspiration can be found from sources as diverse as museums and galleries, books, magazines and street markets.

Now that you have a good understanding of what research is and what it needs to contain in order for it to be useful and relevant, you now need to know where to find this information.

In this chapter we aim to explain how you choose a concept and set a theme that may be narrative, conceptual or abstract. We also explain the differences between primary and secondary sources, as using both in your research will be essential. This chapter also provides in-depth explanations regarding the different sources of inspiration available, from museums and art galleries to the natural world and architecture. This chapter also features interviews with a variety of designers that begin to show how they start a collection and establish themes or concepts, as well as where and how they begin their research.

Choosing a theme or concept

When it comes to choosing a theme for your collection you need to consider that it should be something that firstly responds to the brief, if there is one and secondly, stimulates you to be creative. Words and images may well have been already explored in the brainstorming process and therefore will assist in the collation of ideas into a possible theme or concept.

A theme or concept is the essence of a good collection and is what makes it unique and personal to you. Remember that a good designer will explore aspects of their own personality, interests and viewpoints about the world around them; fusing them into a vibrant, innovative and credible collection.

A theme may be driven by several different approaches. They are as follows:

Abstract

This is where you work perhaps with an unrelated word or description, for example, 'surrealism'.

This word is then translated into a series of ideas or leads the approach to the research and design explored.

What images and words would you associate with surrealism? How might a garment eventually express this word?

'The simplest surrealist act consists of dashing down into the street, pistol in hand, and firing blindly, as fast as you can pull the trigger, into the crowd'

Conceptual

This is where you might explore a variety of unrelated visual sources that can be drawn together because of similar or juxtaposed qualities. For example, a photograph taken of a piece of mineral rock and a shell, alongside a piece of pleated fabric and images of the artist Christo and Jeanne-Claude's installation work, such as wrapping the Reichstag Building in Berlin, Germany with fabric.

This combination of information might also possess similar qualities that could be explored, translating into shapes, textures and colours in the design of your collection.

2

Narrative

Narrative by its definition means a written account of something, perhaps a story or a tale.

The designer John Galliano is famous for creating wonderful stories and characters for his collections, often creating a muse as his central focus, for example, the 1920s' dancer Josephine Baker was inspiration in one collection, as was the Countess de Castiglione. Each of these characters not only brings style, but also a personality and helps to direct the sources of research and the design, as well as the final presentation of the collection.

It is important to remember that regardless of how you start the generation of ideas, it is the clothes that you will ultimately be judged on by the world's fashion buyers and press.

'It's great to tell a story in a collection, but you must never forget that, despite all the fantasy, the thing is about clothes.'

John Galliano, Galliano, Colin McDowell, Weidenfeld & Nicolson

JOSÉPHINE BAKER. -Folies-Bergère-

3

Choosing a theme or concept > What are primary sources?

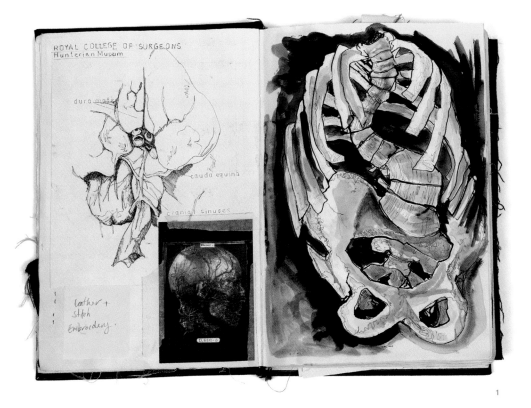

1

2

What are primary sources?

Primary sources are the findings you have collected or recorded first hand. In other words they are the objects you have drawn directly from, for example, anatomical references from a museum of natural history.

Primary sources are generally recorded through drawings or photographs, and often provide greater sensory associations than just the object itself, for example, touch and smell may all recall memories and be included in the final design process.

3

What are secondary sources?

Secondary sources are therefore the findings of other people. These may be found in books, the Internet, journals, and magazines. They are just as important as primary sources of research and often allow you to see and read about things that are no longer around or are not easily accessible.

It is vital that you understand both types of sources and that in any good research there is a balance of both. Primary sources will call upon your drawing talents and secondary will utilise your investigative skills. So be prepared to bring both together in your design research.

1
An example of drawing in a student sketchbook.

2
Examples of drawings in sketchbooks by the designer Richard Sorger.

3
A variety of examples of secondary sources.

Sources of inspiration

1
Sketchbooks demonstrating initial material that has influenced the direction of the design.

2
Sample pages of dedicated fashion websites that are available to browse fashion collections past and present.

You should now understand what research is and the elements it should contain in order for you to design from it. Also explained is the need for a concept or theme. So where do you find the information in order to begin the process of gathering your research?

What are the sources of inspiration?

The Internet

This is probably the easiest place to start, as it is the most accessible way of gathering information, images and text from all over the world. Using search engines to find websites that may be dedicated to the subject you have begun to look at is often the fastest way to find inspiration.

Remember research is not just about visual inspiration, but also the tangible practical things such as fabric sourcing. The Internet allows you to get in touch with companies and manufacturers who may be able to provide you with fabric samples, trimmings and specialist skills in production or finishing.

The Internet also has some great websites dedicated to fashion; www.style.com is fantastic for up-to-date catwalk images of the latest collections from top designers around the world. Having a good 'fashion awareness' is essential if you are to progress within the industry.

Some useful website addresses:

www.costumes.org
www.fashionoffice.org
www.promostyl.com
www.fashion.about.com
www.style.com
www.fashion-era.com
www.wgsn-edu.com
www.londonfashion-week.co.uk
www.premierevision.fr
www.hintmag.com
www.infomat.com
www.pantone.com

2

Libraries, books and journals

A library is a wonderful place to begin your research as it can offer immediate references for images and text in the form of books and journals. A library allows you to explore aisles of books on subjects that you may not have initially considered during your brainstorming sessions. There is something special about leafing through a book; the smell, touch and visual stimulus they can provide are often forgotten when simply looking on the Internet. Books are things that are themselves crafted and designed. Viewing an original manuscript of Victorian drawings is far more inspirational than seeing them on a computer screen.

You should be able to access a library in almost every town and city and it can provide you with a general and broad selection of books. However, if you are studying at college or university then you should have access to a much more specific range of books and journals that will hopefully be more related to you and the courses taught there.

1
Just a small selection of inspirational books.

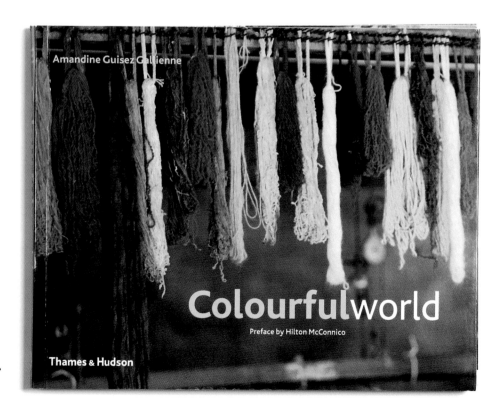

Amandine Guisez Gallienne

Colourfulworld

Preface by Hilton McConnico

Thames & Hudson

Magazines

Knowing your subject and having an awareness of fashion is an essential part of the research process and magazines are a good place to develop this knowledge.

Magazines are a great source of information and potential inspiration for the designer; they can firstly provide you with images of the latest trends, styles and garments from other designers in the industry, and secondly give you insight into other aspects you should consider as a designer, for example, lifestyle and cultural interests that may affect the market you wish to design for.

Looking at other designers' collections is not so that you can copy what they are doing, but to give you an understanding of what has already been created and the possibilities that are open to you. There are so many different magazines out on the news-stands these days that you should not simply gravitate towards the obvious ones, such as *Vogue* and *Elle*. There are many more fashion, art and lifestyle publications that focus on niche markets that you should be aware of. These magazines are filled with new up-and-coming talent and feature not just on the clothes' designers, but also on the art direction, hair and make-up artists, photographers and stylists.

Building your knowledge of designers, trends and lifestyle habits is not something that will happen overnight and should be something that is done regularly over time so that it will help you establish yourself within the industry.

As a student you may well be asked to recall your favourite designers or the publications you read by your tutors as a way of demonstrating your knowledge and interest in the subject. But equally you may be asked to begin market research by using magazines for a design team in a large high street company, so it is important to understand this part of the process at an early stage in your career.

Magazines to investigate: *International Textiles, View, Uomo Book, Wonderland, Fashion, Vogue, In Fashion, Bloom, Another Magazine, View 2, 10.*

1
Knowing your subject: here is a selection of magazine titles you should be aware of.

1

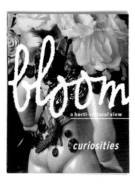

1

2

Museums and art galleries

Museums are a wonderful source of primary research as they contain a huge and diverse array of objects, artefacts and historical treasures. There are often museums dedicated to specific interests, such as the military, science, natural history or the arts.

Places such as the Victoria and Albert museum in London or The Metropolitan Museum of Art in New York are vast palaces of global art, design, history and culture. They offer the designer a wonderful starting point to the research process, enabling you to explore many galleries and rooms dedicated to different subjects, countries and periods. The possibilities are under one roof, but have the potential to be endless.

Art galleries are also an essential part of the research process as they offer inspiration for subject matter, colour, texture, print and surface embellishment. Artists have directly influenced many collections by fashion designers. For example, Versace used Andy Warhol's Marilyn Monroe Pop Art print from the 1960s as the inspiration for a print on a dress. Yves Saint Laurent incorporated Mondrian's graphic work on to a shift dress during the 1960s. And Elsa Schiaparelli worked with the surrealist artist Salvador Dali on many pieces during the 1930s.

But paintings can also provide you with a picture of life and dress from a period or country where photography was not present, for example, Renaissance art and sculpture in Rome or perhaps scriptures from Egyptian times.

Most towns and cities will have a central museum and art gallery, so it is wise to explore what is available as you may find hidden treasures worth further investigation.

3

1–4
Museums and art galleries can provide a wealth of diverse information from which to start your research and design process.

4

Costume

As a fashion designer it is essential that you have a reasonable working knowledge of dress/costume history. If you understand what has been done in the past it allows you to expand from this and take it into the future. Taking inspiration from period dress allows you to exploit old styles of shape, construction, fit, print and embroidery and develop new interpretations of these. With such a rich and diverse dress history there are many references that you can develop into your collection.

Designers like Vivienne Westwood and John Galliano are famous for utilising costume influences in their collections. Places like the Victoria and Albert museum in London and the Fashion Museum in Bath contain wonderful collections of period dress that can be accessed and drawn from in your research.

There are also private archives, such as the ones owned by London College of Fashion and another by the Fashion Institute in New York that can be accessed and are often on display in the galleries. Some local museums may contain small collections of dress history and these often give insight into the people of that town or city. Costume or vintage clothing can also be found or purchased if you know where to look.

1
Modern interpretation of 1920s'-styled dress.

2
Illustration showing characteristics of 1920s'-style flapper girls. Dover Press.

3
Victorian illustration with distinctive leg-of-mutton sleeves. Dover Press.

4
D&G contemporary denim jacket. A contemporary interpretation of the Victorian sleeve shown here.

1

2

4

3

Flea markets and second-hand shops

We have already discussed that research is about poking and prying, sourcing information and always being on the look out for references for design. Flea markets and second-hand shops offer you an ideal opportunity to discover old treasures, discarded artefacts and vintage or period clothes by simply wandering in and around them.

Most of the great fashion capitals of the world have good areas to search for such markets and shops; for example, Portobello Road Market in London, Greenwich Village in New York and Monmartre in Paris.

Some designers have built their individual design identity on using vintage or recycled components in their collections.

1

The famous Portobello Road Market, London.

2–3

Vintage-inspired collection by Robert Cary-Williams A/W06. Catwalking.com.

Travel

As a designer it is important to explore and discover your environment and realise that everything around you has the potential to be research. Therefore the ability to travel must also be an important part of the research process. Looking at and learning from other cultures and countries can provide you with a wealth of information that can be translated into contemporary fashion design.

Large design companies will often send their design team abroad to research for their collections. Gathering old treasures, pieces of fabric, artefacts, garments, jewellery and accessories – anything they think could be used as inspiration. Photographs and drawings are also a vital part of recording the experiences of travelling to another country.

As an aspiring designer it would be important to consider that a holiday abroad could also be an opportunity to gather research.

1

Inspiration board showing examples of world costume and dress.

1

'*Fashion is architecture. It is a matter of proportions.*'

Coco Chanel

Architecture

Fashion and architecture have a great deal in common, it may be surprising to learn. They actually start from the same point, the human body. They both protect and shelter, while they also provide a means to express identity, whether it is personal, political, religious or cultural.

Fashion and architecture also express ideas of space, volume and movement and have parallel practices in the way they exploit materials from flat two-dimensional surfaces to complex three-dimensional forms. It is because of this common factor that architecture is a wonderful subject matter to explore for research as a fashion designer.

Like costume, architecture can express period trends and has often linked itself with social interests, as well as changes in technology, in particular the use of new materials and production techniques.

You only need to look at the work of Gaudi in the late 1800s and early 1900s and his interest in the natural world, and the related art and dress movement it was part of, to see how closely fashion and architecture are linked.

More recently Japanese designers such as Yohji Yamamoto and Comme des Garçon demonstrate clear similarities in the garments they create and the contemporary architecture they are surrounded by.

1
Linear and structural qualities can be seen in the cables of New York's Brooklyn Bridge.

2
The Empire State Building, New York.

3
Decorative features such as the domes of the Brighton Pavilion, inspired by Indian palaces.

The natural world

The natural world provides a vast and diverse source of inspiration for gathering primary information. It is a source of visual stimuli that can inspire all of the key elements you need to determine in your research, such as shapes, structures, colours, patterns and textures.

Your interest may lead you to look at rare birds of paradise or butterflies and insects. It may be that you explore the patterns of snakes or the jungle foliage of a rain forest. The opportunities are endless and as a source of inspiration the natural world is one that is consistently explored by designers.

1–3
Illustration and books referencing the natural world. Illustration courtesy of Dover Press.

4–5
Manish Arora S/S07 tropical bird-inspired embroidered garments.

6
Basso & Brooke S/S07 digitally printed kimono-inspired embroidered cape.

1

2

3

4

5

6

Film, theatre and music

The industries of film, theatre and music have always had very close links to fashion and dress. The famous Hollywood starlets of the 1930s and '40s were always photographed dressed in garments by French designers such as Lanvin, Balenciaga and Dior. The glamorous and unattainable lives they exuded only added to the desire for the clothes they wore and for the designers to create even more fantastic pieces.

But as well as dressing the stars, film and theatre have often influenced what has appeared on the catwalks. Films such as Baz Luhrmann's *Moulin Rouge* helped create a huge interest in corsetry and the burlesque. And most recently the film about Edie Sedgewick starring Sienna Miller,

called *Factory Girl*, has created a buzz about fashion in the 1960s. In more modern times it has been the role of the rock or pop stars to excite and create a lifestyle that people aspire to. Through the clothes and associations with designers and brands, they often promote collections in videos, promos, movies and publications. Vivienne Westwood and Malcolm MacLaren famously dressed the Sex Pistols in the 1970s and started a whole new subculture movement called punk.

Links with music and fashion are today so close that we are now in an era when the big American hip hop and rap stars are creating their own fashion labels, such as Sean John and Rocawear, and promoting them through music.

Because of these close associations the music and film industries are certainly areas you may wish to explore as inspiration, whether it be to start your collection with a muse or look to a movie theme as a direction to research.

1

1
Madonna has been a constant source of influence and inspiration to designers, from Jean Paul Gaultier to Dolce & Gabbana.

2
Baz Luhrmann's *Moulin Rouge* led to a revived interest in corsetry and the burlesque.

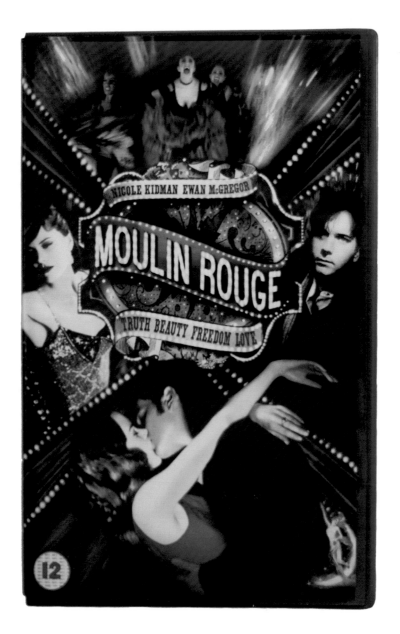

2

1

2

3

Street and youth culture

We have already looked at the importance of contemporary trends and how these are often related to global and cultural interests and changes in taste. And we have referred to the 'bubble-up effect' and how trends can form on the street and influence catwalk designs and ultimately what is fashionable in the mainstream.

It is therefore essential that the research process should include possible inspiration from the street and from subcultures or special interest groups.

Influences may come from trends in clothing styles, for example the Kokeshi kids from Tokyo, the skateboarders from Downtown LA or the club kids from the 1990s in New York.

All of these subculture youth groups have an identity and style of their own and have influenced many designers' collections in the past, from the clothes to the make-up and styling.

By looking to and experiencing the street and what it has to offer at any one moment, in any one city, you can filter out trends and interests and identify what is fresh, new and directional.

But street culture can also be an area to look back on as old street styles have also influenced contemporary designers.

<u>1–3</u>
Tokyo Kokeshi kids demonstrating their individual customised street style.

New technologies

The development of new technologies in the fashion industry is an element that has always played a role in the design and research process.

During the 1960s there was a huge technological breakthrough in synthetic fibres and an interest in space and the future that inspired a generation of young designers, such as Mary Quant, André Courrèges and Pierre Cardin.

More recently there have been technological developments in digital printing.

Designers such as Basso & Brooke and Manish Arora have made full use of these new techniques in their signature prints for their collections. There are also designers such as Issey Miyake, Hussein Chalayan and Junya Watanabe that construct their garments out of a whole new generation of fabrics and materials.

It is important to note that it is not just the creative components that are being subjected to new technological breakthroughs, but also the production and manufacturing industries that support the designers. The use of the computer and the incredible advances it has brought, is just one of the ways in which technology is working to improve, develop and innovate a huge variety of processes within the industry.

As a designer it is important to consider these new technologies and future ones when you are beginning a new collection.

Forecasting and trend agencies

1, 4

Hussein Chalayan A/W07. The use of modern technology has always been prevalent in Chalayan's collections. Catwalking.com.

2

Sarah Arnett A/W07. Digitally engineered print.

3

Examples of forecasting magazines.

Forecasting and trend agencies can also be a possible source of inspiration.

As already discussed, having an awareness of street cultures, new trends, new technologies and global interests is important when it comes to researching for a new collection or the development of a new brand.

Tracking trends is not just about looking at fashion, but also about looking at demographics, behaviour, technologies and lifestyle. Consumer analysis will often help a designer create the right clothes and accessories for people in the future.

Companies will spend huge amounts of their budgets to gain this sort of insight into the market and what they then need to focus their ideas towards.

Fashion forecasting agencies are companies set up to support the industry and specifically look at current trends and cultural pursuits. They are, through market research, able to offer the designer a glimpse into ideas and directions that are becoming popular in society. These ideas can take the form of colours, fabrics, details and shapes, all of which are essential to the creative process as a fashion designer.

The information these agencies produce can be accessed through specialist magazines and trend books, as well as through presentations at trade fairs such as Premier Vision in Paris.

3

2

4

Designer case studies

In this section of the book there is a series of interviews with practising fashion designers and textile specialists.

Each has his or her own approach to the research and design process, but many similarities and evidence of good practice can be drawn from the advice offered in this section.

1   2   3

1–5
Visual references of individual
designer case studies.

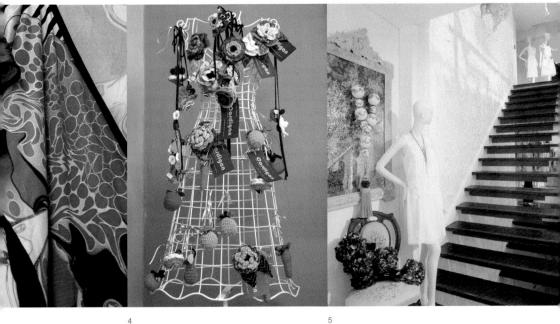

4   5

Sarah Arnett, fashion designer, interview

How do you start the research for a collection?

I try to imagine a muse or character to start the creative process and build an identity to the collection. This character is then considered in every part of the research and design process; 'would she wear this?' is a question I always ask myself. The muse or character could come from a period reference, a contemporary magazine, a book I am reading or a film that I loved at the time. The character is not necessarily someone famous or well known in period literature, but simply a person that captures the spirit of the collection I want to create. The image of the person can also express a set of colours and textures that may inspire me. This season I found a picture of a beautiful Irish model who had dark hair and fair skin and a softness about her. This is then very much a starting point, that first page of the research and things can change as I develop the collection further.

What are your sources of inspiration and research?

My research is documented in a sketchbook and all the influences on me are written down and sketched. I am always looking in magazines, using the Internet, exploring museums and using the research as an opportunity to learn more.

There are however a little gang of 'favourite things' I would like to explore that are always in the back of my mind at the beginning of a season. They may have been stored there for years and perhaps the time is right for them now. So I mix the other more current things that have influenced me with them and some of those other favourite things get put to one side and stored for another time.

www.saraharnett.co.uk

This season I wanted to use a picture I had seen some years ago at an exhibition called 'Earth from above' that was at the Natural History Museum in London. I remembered there was this amazing dark, almost black image of a seascape with an oil slick that shimmered and had this gold iridescent colour to it. This was something that had a big influence on this season's colour palette and prints.

I also love foliage and more often than not will start drawing with leaf shapes and then explore pattern and manipulation on the computer to try to incorporate the variety of influences found at that point.

Once I have initially begun to gather my inspiration, I try to give the collection a title; this season was simply called 'dancing dresses'. I do this as I do not work alone and I have other people that are part of the design process. I find that having a title helps to bring everyone on-board and perhaps start to visualise ideas associated with that title.

What is the next stage in your research process?

The next stage of the process is very practical; I have a meeting that involves the sales agents, sample manager and production team, and we dissect the last collection in terms of what sold, what we could have sold much more of, what was a nightmare in terms of manufacture and so on.

This then helps me focus the ideas I have at this point as I often have so much I want to say and the list of good and bad aspects from the last collection will generally stop any avenues that are not practical.

From this point I start to produce many different ideas for print using a computer, as digital printing on fabric is what I have become associated with in my collections. I love the speed of a computer and the immediacy you have with it as a designer.

Technology has played a huge role in the development of my label because without the use of digital printing the translation of my prints would be impossible.

Digital printing gives me up to four metres to repeat a design, so that allows me to cut a skirt from one end and a top in the other, this means they will have a relationship to each other, but will not be the same and I love that element of the digital design process.

The technology is also continuing to play a role in the development of ideas, as new fabrics are available to print on, so this has an impact on the garment shapes or styles that I can create. Digital printing has for a while only been available on silks and this has meant the design has often been leaning towards eveningwear. But as other qualities become possible you are led into new markets. I am currently working with a silk and wool herringbone that will allow me to develop more tailored pieces for daywear.

How do you start to translate your research into design?

I will often start to develop little drawings and collages in my sketchbook, using printouts from the computer of my textile designs. Then through folding, cutting and drawing on them I am able to see how they may evolve into garment ideas. Sometimes things I print have been engineered specifically for a dress style and this is often explored in the sketchbook and then further on the computer.

The designs will be drawn out as simple line drawings or technical specs and then layered over the prints. This process can often change the original idea as scale and placement suddenly shift for the better as I play with the elements on the screen.

I also love to drape the fabric on the stand once it has been sample printed, and seeing the print on the cloth suddenly opens up new, almost magical potential that I had perhaps not previously considered.

The use of technology and computer design development is really the most vital tool in the translation of research into design and helps me make my mind up before we go into sample development and production, which is the next stage.

1
Sarah Arnett S/S06 (and overleaf) her design studio in Brighton, UK.

Sources of inspiration > Designer case studies

Kate Jenkins, designer and owner of knitwear label Cardigan, interview

Tell me what you do? Describe your business.

Cardigan is a knitwear accessories label whose products range from beautiful handmade wraps and scarves to bags. The other side of the business acts as a knitwear design consultancy to fashion labels worldwide providing new ideas for embroidery, crochet and machine knitting. 2006 saw the opening of Cardigan's first studio shop, which stocks all Cardigan products and regularly holds exhibitions to launch new products. Customers are encouraged to view the studio attached to the shop to see where the designs are made.

How do you start the process for a new collection or series of swatches/scarves? For example, do you sit down with sales figures and decide which products were most successful last season, or who were the biggest clients for a season and what did they like/buy? Do these factors have any impact on your starting point for a new collection?

I generally start the ideas process with lots of knitting as I find it much easier to knit or crochet an idea rather than draw it, as it never comes out as I have intended. This way of design makes it much quicker and easier to translate original ideas and gives me a better understanding of how certain yarns and colours work together. I use the same method for all my embroidery and crochet ideas also. Sometimes a mistake can turn itself into a new idea or technique.

I do listen to buyers and customers as to what they like and to a certain degree this is considered when designing new collections, but I try and come up with a few 'test products' as customers are always looking for something special and unique.

What are your sources of inspiration?

My sources of inspiration come from everywhere. I think it is really important to be aware of lifestyle trends as well as current fashion trends. I look to see what music people listen to, exhibitions that are on, new film releases and of course vintage clothes, antique markets/fairs and my ultimate favourite, car boot sales (weather permitting!), and finally, my vivid imagination, which is always a good source of reference.

www.cardigan.ltd.uk

Do you have research books or mood-boards to help start your research/design process?

I always have a mood-board on the go in the studio and a really big sketchbook filled with bits of fabric, drawings, knitting patterns etc. I think it's important to write down every idea you have, as it's so easy to get carried away and forget things.

Do you design for specific clients in mind or do you create whatever you feel like for that season?

I tend to work on ideas that will create a reaction in people whether it is based on certain colours or their sense of humour. The Cardigan customer is generally a creative individual who isn't a 'current fashion trend follower', but is confident making her own decisions and uses Cardigan accessories to complement her look.

Do you set themes to your collections? Do you group samples into collections?

I sometimes set themes to each collection, but I always return to fauna and flora as it translates perfectly into knitwear and it has become a trademark of Cardigan accessories.

Do you have any advice for someone interested in the industry?

My advice to anyone interested is to work hard and don't be afraid to take risks. Always believe in your product and your capabilities.

1–4
Kate Jenkins for Cardigan. Examples of knitted wraps and crocheted broaches, design studio and shop, Brighton, UK.

Sources of inspiration > Designer case studies

3

4

Winni Lok, knitwear designer and Head of Knitwear at Whistles, interview

In this interview the answers are based on the research and design practice at Whistles, a boutique high-street fashion store.

How do you start the research for a collection?

The new collection is normally inspired by the prints we buy for the season, as well as from books and magazines. The prints may be vintage or from specialist print companies who focus on putting prints together or embellishment panels. From a knitwear point of view, we also have knit swatch companies who we buy from, and these may be inspirational for knit techniques, or styling or again embellishment ideas. Being a 'high-street' company, we also have to be aware of up-and-coming trends; what is happening on the catwalk and in the stores.

For me, research is a very important time of development as it allows you to think about the mood and it sets the precedence for the collection. It is a time to formulate and nurture ideas.

Do you set themes?

Our collection used to be set in groups of stories throughout the season, between seven or eight over the season. This means that with each delivery there was a slightly different theme behind each one. However, we have changed the way we look at the collection for the season and for A/W07, we will be designing the whole season, as a complete collection, as say, a ready-to-wear designer would. This means that the collection will have more continuity throughout the whole collection and what defines the move from autumn through to winter, will be an intensity in the colour palette. Therefore, we hope that when the collection sits in the store, in terms of merchandising, the clothes will sit happily together through the season and hopefully there will be more synergy in the way the stores look. From a customer's point of view, this will make the clothes easier to read from a purchasing point of view.

What kind of brief do you have?

At Whistles, one of our main objectives when we begin designing for the new season is to address the clothing options for the season. This basically means that we have to make sure that the range comprises of a certain amount of styles (or 'options') within each clothing category. This information is provided by the merchandising department, who will tell us, for example, how many coats we need to have, how many styles of knit pieces, dresses and so on. This is based seasonally on the reaction to sales and targets for budgets, etc.

What tend to be your sources of inspiration? Where do the ideas come from? Libraries, travels, museum visits, trend agencies?

I tend to get inspiration from books, galleries, whatever is happening around me on the streets, music...pretty much anything.

Working as a team who is the lead?

There are two Heads of Design within Whistles. I'm the Head of Knitwear and there is also a Head of Woven Fabrics. Then there is the Brand Director, who oversees all of the company. Within the Whistles' team, I will work closely with the Head of Product, who ensures that we get the garments that we want and their job is to liaise with the factories and manage not only the product, but the critical path, which means that we design to a time schedule to guarantee that the product arrives in the store when it should.

www.whistles.co.uk

Who ultimately says yes or no?

Ultimately, that would be our Brand Director, Amanda Burrows. We work closely with her in putting the range together.

Is the research and design process a collaborative thing or individual?

We put the entire collection together as a team. The Heads of Design will think about what we would like for the collection and then we will ask our teams to do the research. With my team, I may ask them to look at vintage shops or books for ideas and maybe ask them to do some swatch ideas with consideration to yarn and texture.

1

3

1–4
Whistles newly designed flagship store interior, St. Christopher's Place, London, UK. Photography by Louise Melchior.

4

Richard Sorger, fashion designer, interview

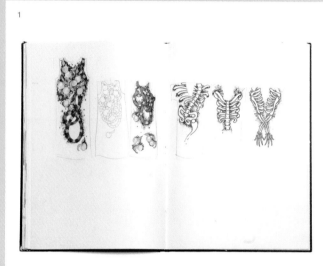

1

Describe your label, what is it about?

I primarily design embroideries – the generic term for beads, sequins, and thread work (embroidery) – which I then place on simple garments. I'm more interested in the imagery of the embroideries than the structure of the clothes – the clothes are a blank 'canvas' to work on. My embroidery designs are quite graphic and figurative rather than 'pretty'. I'd like to think that the designs I produce are in the grand tradition of Lesage, which is the haute couture house of embroidery. Couture embroidery is all about knowing how light hits a garment and lights up a room.

How do you start the research process? Do you start by looking at what sold last season?

When you run your own label you're constantly learning from the mistakes and successes of each season. To begin with I was very concerned at how expensive the pieces were working out at wholesale, but the buyers I've met generally didn't raise an eyebrow. It's always a good idea to have some pieces that have a low entry-level price as you're seeing buyers who have different markets, but I'm lucky that with some of the pieces I don't have to compromise the design because of the cost – my pieces look expensive.

I'm a believer in 'evolution' not 'revolution'; I don't believe in changing everything each season. If a piece or a technique of embroidery has sold well I will be shameless and include it in some form in the next season.

What are your sources of inspiration?

Like most designers I'm constantly on the look out for new inspiration. I produce two collections a year and I often get private commissions and projects for a specific client, so you sometimes have to come up with an idea at the drop of a hat. I regularly visit galleries and museums and some of the things that inspire me can have an effect in an abstract rather than literal way, just a mood or a colour. I also like the thinking behind a lot of contemporary design – furniture and product design. But my main source of inspiration at the moment is natural history. I hate to admit it but I like zoos – the last time I went I got over excited about the vultures and other raptors. But I haven't used them. Yet.

Do you set themes or a narrative to your collections?

I try to, but if a theme gets in the way of a good idea I'm not precious. A collection has to gel as a whole, but rather than doing this through the theme, it can be done through the colour and the techniques that I use.

Do you design with any one in mind?

No. But I've sold to very different markets so I try to include pieces that I think will appeal to different markets/clients.

How do you collate your research?

I collate imagery in a sketchbook along with drawings and designs. I also put images, fabric etc. on a wall in my studio – things that inspire me but don't necessarily have a relevance to the collection that I'm working on. And I try to have a clear out every six months. I clear the wall and start again.

How important is the research to the design process for you?

Research is the best bit! Research is the point of unlimited possibilities. I get excited about what I'm potentially going to do and hunting down the right book, the right photograph, the right angle of an animal to draw from, is a challenge I relish.

1
Design sketchbook illustrating early drawings for skeleton bead work as seen on the garment.

2
Finished beaded and embroidered garments.

1

2

How do you start the design process from the research?

After the optimism of the research there's the pessimism of the initial design work. It takes a while to 'hit' the designs that I know will work and that satisfy me. And it's a stage I go through each time I sit down to design a collection, so I always try to remind myself that it's only a phase and that I'll 'break through'. So far I've been right.

With a collection that uses a variety of images I find it really helps me to draw the subject matter. It's a pleasure to draw and it's also when I learn how to draw, for example, the curve of a snake's head from different angles or the line of a piece of fairground 'flash' artwork. I can't just sit down with a garment pattern in front of me and convincingly draw a line without the initial sketchbook work. It's also a time when I can process in my mind the research that I've gathered and it buys me time to think about what I might do with the actual designs.

How do you develop your designs into a collection?

I make sure that colours, fabrics, imagery and techniques are repeated within the collection, but generally what holds my collections together is the fact that everything is embroidered.

Do you have any advice to anyone interested in the industry?

Some formal training is useful. There are exceptions to the rule, successful designers who haven't trained at college, but these come along about once every few generations and generally fashion designers benefit from having done a Degree or Masters.

Get as much work experience as you're (financially) able to do – a job offer can often come from making yourself indispensable within a design house and even if it doesn't, it's experience to put on your CV.

Don't be in a rush to set up your own label, make contacts and learn from other people's mistakes. It can also help if you're a 'niche' designer – if you design tailoring, accessories, or knitwear, for example, a buyer will know to come to you, rather than a designer who does a bit of everything and not much of anything. But this can also work to your disadvantage if a buyer isn't interested in your specialty.

And it really helps if you're sociable, energetic, and organised.

3

<u>1</u>
Sketchbook showing early drawings.

<u>2</u>
Finished interpreted design featuring a beaded King snake motif.

<u>3</u>
Bird of Paradise-inspired embroidery and bead work.

Julien Macdonald, fashion designer, interview

How do you start the research process for a new collection?

Because it is my own company I am lucky enough to have the freedom to explore and develop my research and ideas without too many constraints. The main thing that I consider is cost. This is one of the most important things to the buyers, as they will not pay more than they have to for certain styles. There is a European guide that all fashion houses go by that sets a maximum price that customers will pay for certain items like a dress. I will sit and discuss with sales what sold well last season and speak with the production team to see if we had any difficulties. And that is really all, from then on it is very much down to me to decide what I want to achieve with the collection.

What are your sources of inspiration?

I love to travel and when I have the time I will go and visit many of the great museums of the world and see any particular exhibitions that may be being held. I believe it is important to go and visit the different countries where I sell in order that I can better design with them in mind. I love going to the Metropolitan museum in New York, the Louvre in Paris, and the Victoria and Albert museum in London. I often get the V&A to open up some of their archives for me so I can view perhaps a Madame Grès dress or an amazing textile. My studio is based in Portobello Road in London and I love to go and see what is in the market on Fridays. I love looking at vintage clothes and, as well as using the V&A, when I can I go to the Angels costume archives on the outskirts of London. This is an amazing place that has thousands of costumes from all the Hollywood

films and is used by many designers and couture houses including Mark Jacobs and Givenchy. It is an expensive resource, but it is vast and diverse in what you can find, from showgirl costumes to Harry Potter costumes.

I love using books and old magazines. I particularly love looking at old Italian and American Vogue magazines from the 1970s. For my summer collection I was looking at Matisse and his cut-out paintings as inspiration for print, these were then mixed with orchid photographs taken by Robert Mapplethorpe and then digitally manipulated by a print designer.

Do you ever design a collection with one person in mind?

Not really, I think that the idea of designing to a specific muse can be dangerous as you can in fact alienate some of your potential global market. An actress may not be as popular in Dubai as she is in America. And many of the actresses want the freedom to wear many different designers and not necessarily be locked into a contract with one design house. I do however think of people like Marilyn Monroe, who I love, and the types of glamorous women of that Hollywood age.

1

Do you set themes to your collections?

I do like to have themes in what I do, but I don't like them to be obvious references as women want clothes that can be worn and not just presented on a catwalk. So if I wanted to do something with Egyptian art, as this is something I love, I would not then want to style it in that way.

How do you collate your research?

I tend to have storyboards in my studio and these are normally grouped, so I will have inspiration for jersey pieces and then a story for chiffons, dresses and tailoring. There is always a reference for print as this is really the most important part of the collection, as this will often lead all of the design.

How do you start the design process from the research?

The factory will often give me very specific requirements on what they want to see, for example, three dresses, one long, two short, a satin skirt, four blouses etc. and so from this checklist I can begin to explore ideas within the collection. I do a series of preliminary sketches for each of the storyboards and then from these pick up on running themes or techniques, such as a beautiful idea for embroidery or technical detail that can be developed through several garments in a variety of ways or colours. I very rarely work on the stand, but will develop ideas further when I do the fittings and sometimes will change the look of a garment completely at this stage.

1
Privately commissioned Julien Macdonald wedding dress.

2
A/W05 Naomi Campbell, a favourite model of Julien's, in a gold, sequinned evening dress. Catwalking.com.

3
Julien Macdonald takes to the catwalk for his S/S06 collection to rapturous applause. Catwalking.com.

<u>1</u>
Handmade leather-bound
student sketchbook.

'As a fashion designer, I was aware that I was not an
artist, because I was creating something that was made
to be sold, marketed, used and ultimately discarded.'

Tom Ford, fashion designer

So far you have discovered what research is and why
you need it as a designer. You have also learnt where you
can find it and the many sources of inspiration that are
available to you.

In this chapter we aim to explain how you piece together
the information you have found. The format of a sketchbook
is explained and different approaches to compiling your
research, from drawing and collage to deconstruction and
analysis, are examined.

The chapter uses different examples of sketchbook work to
illustrate the many styles you can adopt. It also discusses
how to move the research forward and begin to focus on
key elements on mood- and concept-boards, in preparation
for the design process.

1

The sketchbook

How to compile your research

1–3

Walls of research inspiration at Sarah Arnett's studio and Noki's workshop.

4

Student sketchbook.

As a designer it is essential to explore and experiment with the idea of a sketchbook and how you compile your research.

A sketchbook is generally the place where you can collate and process all the information you have collected and it can become a very personal and individual space for ideas.

1

2

3

Research can also be presented as a series of storyboards. This is often the approach in a design studio, where images, photographs, drawings, fabrics and trimmings are stuck to a wall of inspiration or a series of mood-boards.

Sketchbooks can be purchased brand new in a wide variety of sizes, weights of paper, colours and bindings. They can also be something that you make for yourself, allowing you to work on different qualities of paper, edit and order the work, before binding it. A sketchbook can also be created in a second-hand format, by working in an old novel or textbook, perhaps using the text as a background to the theme of the research.

4

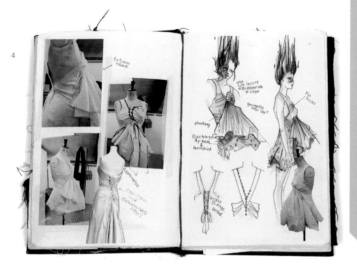

The sketchbook is not just for your own personal use, but can also be a tool to describe and illustrate a collection, and the journey you have taken, to others.

This is often essential information to your tutor, as it will show how you think and perceive the world around you, as well as demonstrating your ability to be a creative thinker. It is also information that can be shared with others in a design studio so that you are all working to a common set of themes, for example, a textile designer, pattern cutter and a stylist.

Research books are not merely scrapbooks filled with tear sheets and photographs, but a place of learning, recording and processing information. A sketchbook should also begin to explore and experiment with a variety of ways in which the information can be presented.

The sketchbook > Drawing

Drawing

Drawing is a fundamental process and skill that you must explore and perfect. It is an ideal way to record information on the spot; in other words, it is a good way to gather primary research.

By using a variety of different drawing media, for example, pencils, inks and paints, you are able to exploit the qualities and styles of line, texture, tone and colour that can be gained from your sources of inspiration and add depth to your research and design.

To draw the whole or part of an object or picture you have sourced helps you to understand the shapes and forms that are contained within it, which, in turn, enables you to translate these lines into a design or when cutting a pattern. Brush marks and textures explored through drawing may also translate into fabric references in your designs.

Understanding and developing your visual language skills is something you will continue to do throughout the creative research process and drawing is just one part of that.

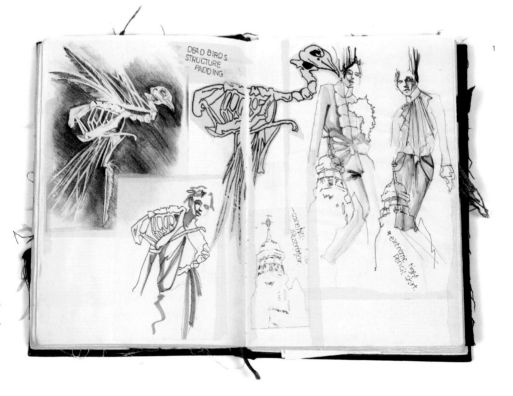

1

Collage

The use of collage in your research is another approach to collating information from different sources, for example, photographs, magazine cuttings and printouts from the Internet.

The images you select need not necessarily have anything immediately in common.

A good collage will explore a variety of elements that have their own strengths and qualities, but in combining them present new directions as a whole. When you are working with images, do not be restricted by the shape, for example, a rectangle or square, cut out the shapes and collage together in a creative way. Think of Monty Python's collaged titles and the work of pop artist Peter Blake, who created the album cover for The Beatles' *Sgt. Pepper's Lonely Hearts Club Band*, when putting the information together. Scale, placement and selection are skills you will start to learn as you explore this technique in your sketchbook.

Collage is described as the artistic composition of sticking bits of paper and photographs to a surface; but the word originally derived from the French word for 'gluing'.

3

2

Juxtaposition

Juxtapose: Place or deal with close together for contrasting effect. Origin mid 19th cent. (earlier (Middle English) as *juxtaposition*): from French *juxtaposer*, from Latin *juxta* 'next' + French *poser* 'to place'.

Oxford Dictionary of English

If collage is about cutting and sticking images together to create new ideas, then juxtaposition is where you place images and fabrics side by side on the page.

It is a method that can often bring disparate elements together that share similarities even though they are different. For example, the spiral shape of an ammonite fossil and a spiral staircase, or the images may be suggestive of a fabric quality, for example, the muscle textures of the human anatomy and a knitted fabric.

1

Inspiration board demonstrating the use of juxtaposition.

2

Student sketchbook showing clear connections between anatomical drawings and knitted textiles.

3

Student sketchbook illustrating the use of deconstruction.

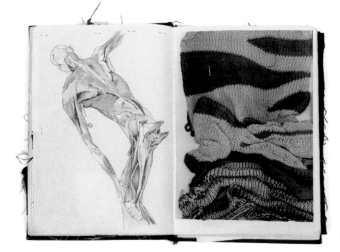

1

2

Deconstruction

To deconstruct or disassemble your research is to consider looking at the information with a new viewpoint. It may simply mean using a viewfinder and drawing an aspect of the object so that you focus on a detail to arrive at an abstract idea from the original source. But it may also mean breaking the information up like a jigsaw puzzle and reassembling it differently to create new lines, shapes and abstract forms to work from.

Disassemble is also a process that relates to working with actual garments as a source of inspiration. It is a technique where you can take existing clothes apart and analyse how they have been created, perhaps taking patterns from them and looking at the construction details that could be translated into your own design ideas.

This method of research will be discussed more in-depth in chapter four.

A viewfinder is a creative tool that allows you to conceal an object and then expose or view only a part of it. It can be made from a simple piece of card or paper and all you need to do is cut a small square window into the centre of it. The window can be as small or as large as you wish, but the point is to offer you a view of only part of the object or image you have sourced.

3

Cross-referencing

1–3

Research boards demonstrating
a variety of cross-referenced
sources.

Your research initially may be quite abstract and varied, with many seemingly unrelated references sourced and explored. Methods like drawing, collage and juxtaposition are great for collating and experimenting with information, but cross-referencing your research is a technique that gets you to look for related visual references or ones that complement each other. These can then be grouped into early themes or concepts for you to explore further in the design process.

The examples show how a Nuam Gabo sculpture and an Issey Miyake garment have similar qualities, as do the pleated texture of shells and the pleats within the Christo & Jeanne-Claude installation art pieces. All of these references come from different sources, but by bringing them together you can see how they relate to one another and form new directions for you to design from.

It is this mix of sources with similar qualities that is the essence of cross-referencing and an essential part of any good research and the early analysis of it.

2

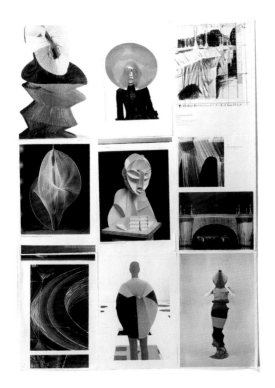

3

Analysis of research

How to compile your research

1

Sketchbook by Richard Sorger demonstrating research and analysis into fabric and beading detail.

2

Student sketchbook exploring draped textures and armour-inspired seams from researched images.

As you begin to explore your research and compile ideas and concepts through collage and cross-referencing you will start to see a potential direction for your design. As we have already discussed, you must have information regarding shapes, textures, details, colour, print and perhaps historical references as part of the research. So it is now important to begin to use your research and analyse it in terms of early design sketches.

Early analysis requires you to draw shapes from the sources you have explored, experimenting with mixed-media sketches, close-up and silhouette studies, linear drawings and details for construction.

These sketches should also explore ideas for texture, pattern and possible embellishments. The drawings need not necessarily be done on a figure and can simply be interpretations of the information you have collected.

Colour should be something that is considered and explored through the use of mixed media, using the research as inspiration and extracting out possible ideas for colour palettes and combinations.

1

The research should have contained some early ideas of texture and possible fabric manipulation and therefore these should form part of the early analysis for fabric design. You must begin to source and edit samples and trims that perhaps have similar qualities to the inspiration and show how your research has informed your thought process into textural fabric ideas.

Another key stage of analysis is to try and translate early shapes from your research into quarter-scale pattern experiments or modelling on a stand. This is a three-dimensional approach to analysis, and by experimenting and translating information gathered, you will begin to see the potential for garment ideas and record this through photography and sketching.

This is an extremely valuable part of the research and design process and one that is given a dedicated chapter to explain further.

2

Focus on key elements

Through the stages of research, compilation and analysis you will
start to have a much clearer direction and focus for your design
concept. Each of these stages will have given you important
inspiration and information to work with as a designer. The analysis
will have drawn out some of the key elements you must consider
when designing a collection, such as shape, colour, fabrics,
details, print and embellishments.

This next stage is simply about focusing your mind using your
sketchbook and creating a series of pages that clearly identify
the elements you wish to work from.

This focus also allows other people to interact with your vision,
in other words, if you were working as a team this is the point at
which other members of the team could respond to the direction
the collection research was taking and add their input or suggestions.

This focusing of the key elements can also be presented as a
series of mood-boards, storyboards or concept-boards.

1

2

Mood-, story-, and concept-boards

The key elements that a mood-board should contain are:

Colour palette: Colours need to be clearly identified through the use of swatches of colour. These can be paint shade cards, Pantone shade cards or could be mixed by you. It is important to present an image that complements and supports the colours you have selected.

Reference to theme/ research: This is to show the viewer where you have come from in the journey of your research. It needs to focus and edit back to the most important images used for your inspiration; for example, if you have explored styles from the 1920s then there should be images that suggest this.

Fabric: During the research process you should have begun to collect fabric swatches and ideas for print, embellishment, trims etc. The mood-board needs to have suggested samples on it to support the developing ideas.

Key words and text: It often helps to have descriptive words or short paragraphs of text that help to describe the theme or story of the collection.

Mood-, story- and concept-boards, as already mentioned are a way of presenting focused design information to others, whether they be your clients, financial backers, team of designers or your tutors.

These boards can be described as the front cover to your collection and should tell the story of your research by presenting a few selected pieces of information. Their very name suggests what they are trying to do, create a mood, tell a story and explore a concept.

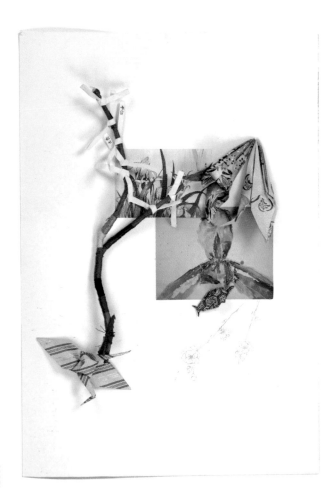

The presentation of this information as the name suggests is generally on board or mount card, as this is a durable format.

The size will be dependent on the use as they are often large scale when used in a design studio, but could be smaller for academic use.

Simple layout and composition of images and fabric swatches is all that is needed and you can even use the techniques explored in research collation as a way of presenting ideas, for example, collage and juxtaposition (seen earlier in this chapter).

Market: Right at the start of your research you should have considered whom you are designing for as a result of the brief you are answering. In terms of the mood-board it would be important to suggest the client in the images, in other words, present images that might reflect their perceived lifestyle or simply use the brand's logo, for example, Whistles or Diesel.

Styling imagery: This is very closely linked to the market as styling imagery helps present your designs within a lifestyle context. Images selected can bring an ideal character to the collection. But it also presents a whole package, in other words, the environment or landscape that the photograph has been taken in, the colours, props and styling, hairand make up, all may well contribute to creating an ideal image for your collection.

1–2

Examples of mood-boards and storyboards.

Focus on key elements > Mood-, story-, and concept-boards > Examples of layout and composition

Examples of layout and composition

1–3

Examples of student sketchbooks showing various forms of layout and composition.

There are no hard and fast rules on how to lay out your research in your sketchbook. You do not need to cover every part of the page with your research and drawings, often the negative space adds to the dynamism of a page and how it is read. Different edges and irregular sizes can all add to the composition and layout of the information. Allow the different sources to interact through collage, but also have space in the juxtaposition layout.

Often a wonderful drawing and a single photograph is all that is needed across a double page to explain an idea and present something visually stimulating. The sketchbook should be about balance and so have quiet and busy moments in terms of information and sources of inspiration.

Ultimately the sketchbook is about inspiration and exploration, so it should never be so preciously laid out as to restrict these essential practices.

Here are some examples of different sketchbook pages that explore further the ideas discussed in this chapter.

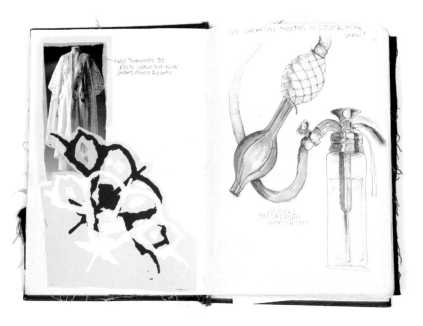

1–2

Further examples of layout and
composition using collage.

Mood-, story-, and concept-boards > **Examples of layout and composition**

1

Student sketchbook focusing on colour and print influences.

2–3

Student sketchbooks showing early exploratory design analysis sketching and use of collage.

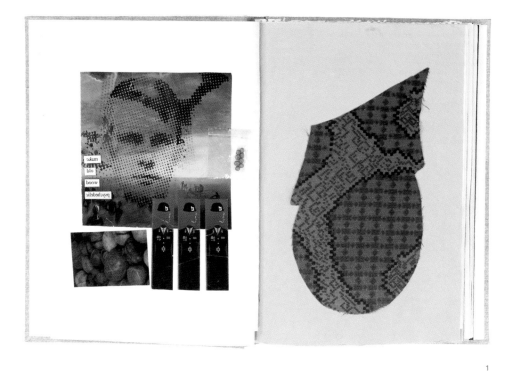

1

2

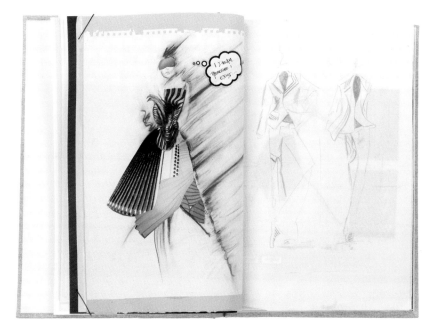

3

'Learn through action.'

Vivienne Westwood, Claire Wilcox, V&A Publishing

1
Viktor & Rolf, *Balls*, 1998 dress,
S/S98. Groninger Museum.

In this chapter we aim to explain the three-dimensional
approaches to research and design and how you can
translate early ideas from your research into shapes and
structures on the body, using model and drape techniques.

As we move into the area of garment development and
design it is essential that you have a basic understanding of
fabric and its different qualities. As a result, in this chapter
there is a brief description of the different types of fibres
and fabrics associated with them.

This chapter also introduces the possibilities of recycled
fashion and working with existing garments as a way of
not only creating ideas on the stand, but also sustainable
fashion pieces. The design label Noki is a pioneer in this
field and he is interviewed for this book about how he
creates a collection.

Model and drape

Volume: In fashion terms this relates to excess fabric in a garment; a garment said to have volume often moves away from the natural curves of the body, creating new silhouettes.

1
Student sketchbook exploring model-and-drape techniques and development into early design sketching.

2
Viktor & Rolf, *Knots*, 1998 dress, S/S98. In this picture you can see clearly how modelling and draping techniques have inspired this dress. Groninger Museum.

3
Student toile further demonstrating the use of gathers and draping on the stand.

Model and drape is a process of creating patterns and garment shapes through manipulating fabric on the stand or mannequin. Folding, pleating, gathering and draping a fabric on to a three-dimensional stand allows a designer to work on more complex shapes and techniques that are often too difficult to develop in the more conventional manner of flat pattern cutting. Draping fabric does not require the aid of a pattern to create designs, but you can choose to incorporate part of an existing pattern in the preparation.

Draping fabric at this stage of the design process is a wonderful way to start early translation of ideas gathered through your research. Taking abstract shapes from what has inspired you and exploring the potential on a mannequin is a much more expressive way of developing ideas for garments than drawing alone, it can be described as akin to sculpting fabric on to the body.

Draping on the stand is also a technique that can help you begin to understand the relationship between a design sketch and a three-dimensional form. It is often difficult to see how a two-dimensional drawing will translate on to the body and so modelling on a stand can begin to explore the idea more clearly.

It is important when using this technique to still be aware of the body and how the fabric relates to it: volume and shape are important, but does the shape flatter the natural contours of the body?

Recording the work on the stand is equally important, drawing and photographing the ideas as they grow and change is an integral part of the early stages of design development and should form an important part of the design aspect of the sketchbook.

Draping, by its very definition is about fabric, folds and movement, so it is essential that you have a basic understanding of a fabric's qualities and characteristics.

The quality, weight, structure and handle will all play an important part in how something looks and reacts on the stand in the model-and-drape process.

'*It's more like engineering than anything else. It's finding the limits of what you can do when wrapping the body in fabric. Everything evolves. Nothing is strictly defined.*'

John Galliano, Galliano, Colin McDowell

1

2

3

Fibre and fabric qualities

1

Fabric shop interior displaying a range of different material.

2

Michiko Koshino synthetic, inflatable, puffa-inspired jacket.

3

Simon Seivewright A/W95. Pure wool woven dog-tooth jacket.

We have already discussed the importance of researching textures and ideas that could translate into fabric in the first few chapters, and as you start to look more closely at using fabric in your designs it is essential that you have a brief understanding of the properties and qualities of different fabrics.

The choice of fabric for a garment is often essential to its success. The weight and handle of a fabric will decide on the way that the garment hangs and falls on the body. The silhouette is often affected by the quality of fabric used, for example, a silk jersey will naturally drape and flow around the body, whereas a heavier wool will have more structure and create more volume and shape.

Fabric selection is also about function and performance, in other words, is it fit for the purpose required? For example, denim fabric is used in jeans and workwear because of its hardwearing qualities, while Teflon-coated cotton is often used in rainproof and sportswear clothing.

Fabrics are also selected for their aesthetic qualities, in other words how they look, feel and support the creative direction you have chosen, whether it be through print, texture or embellishment.

1

2

3

Here is a brief description of some terms you may come across when dealing with fabrics:

Fibre

Fibre or yarn is the raw material out of which a textile is created and there are three main categories: animal (protein), vegetable or plant (cellulose) and mineral (synthetics). The fibre or yarn is then used to create fabric through either weaving or knitting it together.

Cellulose fibre

Cotton is a good example of a plant fibre or cellulose fabric. The soft 'cotton candy' fibre grows around the seed of the plant and is gathered, processed and spun. It has very versatile qualities as it can be woven and knitted and produced in many different weights, for example, denim cotton and cotton voile. It is naturally breathable and absorbs moisture well, which makes it a good cloth for hot climates or the summer season.

Protein fibre

Protein is an essential component of all living cells and 'Keratin' comes from hair fibres and is the most commonly used protein in the production of textiles.

Sheep and goats are the biggest suppliers of wool fleece, which is the raw product used to create woollen fabrics. Wool is a wonderful warm and slightly elastic fibre that again can be woven or knitted to create cloth. Because of

Model and drape > **Fibre and fabric qualities** > Recycled garment manipulation

its natural origins it is breathable and durable, and it can also be created in many different weights of cloth for different purposes, from tailored suiting to brushed mohair or angora for knitwear.

Silk is also a fibre derived from an animal, the silkworm. It is collected from the cocoon of the silkworm, which is formed from the continuous thread that it wraps around itself for protection. Because of the way it is harvested, silk has always been a fabric associated with wealth and power. The fibre has lustre to it and can be woven in many different weights and finishes.

Man-made fibres and synthetics

These fibres come in two forms, cellulosic and non-cellulosic. The cellulose fibres are created by extracting cellulose from plants and trees and forming fibres such as rayon, Tencel and acetate.

The non-cellulosic fibres are all fibres that are created completely from chemicals and contain no natural fibres. These are known as the synthetics and comprise of fibres such as Lycra, nylon and polyester. The properties that these fibres can bring to fabrics are durability, stretch and water resistance and are often used in sportswear.

1
A selection of synthetic fabric swatches.

2, 4
All Saints menswear pure wool knitted cardigan. Detail showing cable pattern.

3
Simon Seivewright A/W95. Pure wool woven tartan plaid jacket.

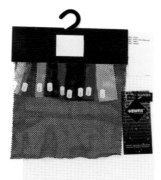

1

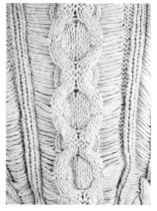

2

3

They are perhaps best used when they are blended with the natural fibres, such as a polycotton and Lycra and wool together.

Woven fabrics

Woven fabrics are created by interlacing vertical yarns (the warp) with horizontal yarns (the weft) at right angles to each other. The tightness and weight of the cloth will depend on how many threads per centimetre there are and the thickness of the yarn.

Knitted fabrics

Knitted fabrics are formed by linked loops of yarn: horizontal rows are called courses and vertical rows are called wales. The elasticity of knitted or jersey fabric gives good stretch and draping qualities.

Non-woven fabrics

These fabrics are produced by the techniques of bonding and felting. Using heat, compression, friction and chemicals, fabrics are created that do not fray, are waterproof, do not tear and can be recycled. Leather and fur can also be classed as non-woven fabrics although they are not man-made.

Other fabrics

These cannot be classified in any of the other areas and are essentially craft techniques, such as lace, macramé and crochet.

Model and drape > **Fibre and fabric qualities** > Recycled garment manipulation

Recycled garment manipulation

1
Noki corset using recycled
components.

2
Noki customised garment.

3
The world of Noki and its creator,
J. J. Hudson.

We have already looked at the idea of modelling and draping on the stand with fabric as a way of translating ideas from your research into early shapes and garment ideas. We have also discussed the different fabric qualities that you should start to familiarise yourself with, how they can be draped on the stand and how they will affect a design.

One final way of developing research and design ideas three-dimensionally is to explore the potential of recycling garments through draping and manipulating them on to a mannequin or stand. By starting to play with these found items on the stand – folding, draping, pinning, cutting and combining them – you will get more information and creative potential from them.

You may well have explored vintage garment stores, charity shops and markets such as Portobello in London as part of your initial research. Using found garments in this process is a key part of successfully interpreting this research into early design ideas.

Working with existing garments can also provide knowledge and skills about how something was made; disassembling a garment and reconstructing it in new ways will help the design process and your understanding of pattern construction. The ideas you create on the stand should be recorded and used to potentially create patterns. But in some cases you may choose to use the actual recycled garments themselves as the finished piece.

There are some designers who have used this vintage recycling and drapery in their collections and one of the best known is the design label called Noki.

Noki, designer at work interview

How did you get started with the whole idea of using rag or recycled garments as a way of designing?

The initial idea behind Noki was as a magazine idea called *NOKI-POD* back in 1996, where the pages were to be an artistic visual aid subverting the message of advertising by providing a beautiful picture rather than the generic commercial visuals you got in the normal magazine format back then, with the branding message put as listings at the back in the small print. This never worked out so keeping the idea and energy I had created I put it into subverting the branded message, shape and function of the not-so-humble T-shirt.

Do you have a political statement or ethical statement to make with your work?

There is definitely a political edge to Noki, but not so much directed towards the government, it is more about the power that the super brands have over our consumerist ways through creating subliminal need through multimedia advertising. This awareness I achieved through working at MTV, Camden as a stylist for the presenters. It was not until I had read the book *Culture Jamming* by Kalle Lassen that I realised how much power the modern brand actually has over our lives through advertising. I just felt a need to create a contemporary statement that did not alienate myself as a lover of brand design and imagery, but perhaps use the brands left-over products and brand itself as an artistic Noki statement of 'one-off'.

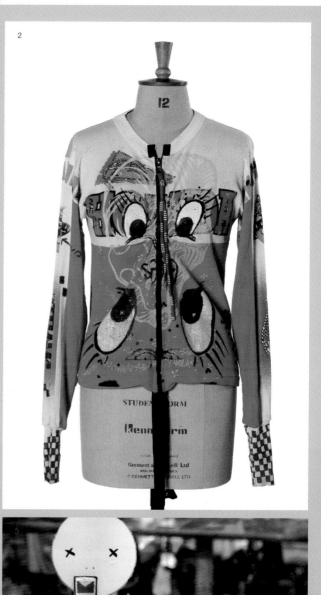

2

3

Do you always start the design process with recycled garments?

When I first started creating Noki customisation it was all about the brand print on the front and how cracked it was, followed by the state of the fabric. The more washed out the better, especially black as it reminded me of a dusty layering, as if 'The Bomb' had gone off and the fall-out had settled on the garment. It was a kind of reflection on how my mind had shifted to be able to think these left-of-centre ideas, which are now seen as normal aesthetics associated with the 'customised' look. At first I was just making Noki-Ts, then I started sewing them together as if I was making a magazine out of them and the brand image was the picture on the page, this created the Noki-Frock. Once Anna Coburn, stylist and David Sims, photographer, started featuring the garments in top-end magazines it encouraged me to experiment more with other garments and Noki fashion history evolved. All the shapes I have evolved through Noki are created by studying the garments and seeing how I can cleverly manipulate them, like the super brands do to us!

There is a very positive paranoid awareness that runs through Noki creativity, every hole punch, cut and slash is a subliminal anarchy. In the mid '90s there was a mass amount of violent anarchy emanating from a very youthful movement against the corporate power that achieved great things for the manufacturers of CCTV equipment. I feel this corporate frustration, but I have a passive aggressive personality so as an artist I would rather creatively make my statement through these ideas in Noki.

You could say that the Noki client is wearing something like a smashed McDonald's window.

Do you find this way of working more creative than pattern cutting?

I studied fashion design at Edinburgh College of Art and passed only on the fact my final collection was very innovative in concept; the rest of the four-year course was a total lie and pattern cutting was total hell for me. I just could not understand it and thought 'fashion designing' was just not for me, but I knew the medium of fashion was. So now being an artist that collages fashion together, I feel that this has achieved a good understanding and balance of the two.

Have you ever taken something from the stand that you have modelled in rag and then recreated it in another fabric?

I have never done this as I have no affinity to pattern cutting, but I have reproduced more pieces under the same creative process to see how other fabrics react under the same treatment, this has created some even better creations so it's pattern cutting of a sorts, as it gets me to similar conclusions.

Do you have a research process?

The only research I need is to know it has come from a second-hand /dead-stock source, the rest of the Noki process just flows from manipulating the product into a different way of looking at it.

There is however a very strong lean towards colour then texture, if something does not feel right to the touch a potential client will reject the piece again. So a sort of research has taken place by knowing what the client will accept.

What inspires you to design and what are your sources of inspiration?

When I am making Noki I don't feel like I am designing anything. What it feels like is creating an object that will attract the eye and to see something new in it. Remember I have just taken it out of the bin, so it was near to destruction. By redefining beauty and adding longevity to a product that was created to be part of a consumerist wasteful society, I am subverting the initial intent the product makers wanted us as a society to buy into. When Noki is worn or desired by a potential client, I feel inspiration has been achieved.

Do you have themes or running ideas through your work? Or is everything stand-alone or one-off?

Everything is all about pushing the concept of creating a new kind of brand value. To buy into Noki is to buy into 'one-off', something the super brands by definition just cannot do, they have to create multiples to survive. This need to homogenise society has created billions of tonnes of waste that sits doing nothing except to remind us of our wasteful ways and consumerist need to spend.

Noki is a modern paradox, created from this very standpoint and a realisation that certain fashion design has come to its logical conclusion. Customisation is my art, it just so happens that it can be worn so it becomes dummed down into just another fashion garment, but this garment happens to have lived again and its structure or DNA changed, so when it is rejected as just another trend its reinvention back into the fashion system will define an era called customisation.

How do you see your work fitting into the industry?

It has already fitted into the industry; there are plenty of old and new brands out there that have been heavily influenced by Noki. They have embraced it as a youthful trend and created a whole new visual language Noki could never have achieved alone. It's called a 'mashup style'; prints over print with embroideries, holes, cuts, slashes and over dyes. In 2007 Louis Vuitton had a mélange of different bits of bags, all stuck together to produce what they called their patchwork tribute and they charged £23,484! So I think something that was once looked down upon back in its days is now looked up to in many a fashion publication for inspiration.

1–3

Examples of Noki garments and footwear.

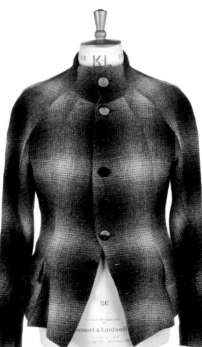

Examples of different
womenswear tailored jackets
by Vivienne Westwood and
Simon Seivewright.

*'Fashion is a form of ugliness so intolerable that we
have to alter it every six months.'*

Oscar Wilde, 1854–1900

Designing is about mixing up known elements in new and
exciting ways in order to create fresh and original products.
It is also about exploiting the full potential from the in-depth
research gathered and translating this successfully. In this
chapter we aim to explain the fundamental stages of
translating research into design. Understanding what the
design development processes are and how they affect
the creative outcomes is essential to being a successful
fashion designer.

This chapter will further explore the silhouette and function of
a garment and look at the choice of fabric and use of colour
and print. It will also provide you with several exercises to
help you generate design ideas and evolve a collection.
The final stages of the design process will be to refine and
edit your ideas to create a cohesive and complete collection.

Bridging the gap

1

Student sketchbook showing collage on figure related to research.

2

Examples of collage on simple templated figure with design drawing progression.

So far all the work you have explored has been focused on the research and inspiration for the design process, gathering ideas and experimenting with information in your sketchbooks, but what about the design? How do you start to design and to bridge the gap between the inspiration and the actual design process?

Certainly working on the stand using the model-and-drape technique will provide you with some key ideas for shape and silhouette that can be used in the early translation of research into design. But there are two other approaches that you should consider in helping you to bridge the gap and start the design process. These are collaged research on figures and photomontage with drapery.

Women artists saw surrealism as a close analysis of their own individuality and allowed their work to reveal many of the complexities and problems inherent with gender designated roles in society

1

Collaged research on figures

This is a very quick and quite literal way to translate your research into design ideas and not one that is really used in industry very often; but it is an ideal technique to try as a novice designer.

It will require you to make several copies of different pages of your research, use a photocopier or scanner to help you with this stage. You will then need to draw out a series of fashion figures or templates (these will be discussed in chapter six) on to layout paper or directly into your sketchbook. You can then simply begin to cut and collage different aspects of your research that you have copied, directly on to the figures. This technique allows you to see immediately the design potential of some of the images. Perhaps spiral shells translate into the shape of a skirt or floral leaves into a dress.

The technique does require you to consider several anchor points on the body, which you need to start to develop your collages from, these are:

- Neck
- Shoulders
- Bust
- Waist
- Hips

Arms and legs should also be given consideration as points to develop from, i.e. sleeves and trousers.

This technique concentrates essentially on the possibilities of shapes and silhouettes on the body, but may also suggest colour, print and texture depending on the research images used in this process.

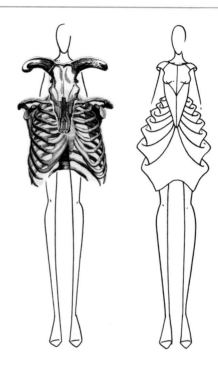

2

Layout paper: This is slightly transparent paper that can be used with templates to draw design development ideas quickly, as you can trace off the figure quickly each time and overlay other ideas. It does not work well with wet media, as it tends to buckle.

Photomontage with drapery

This technique expands on the three-dimensional experiments that you began to explore on the stand. The photographs and drawings of these experiments can now be used on a two-dimensional figure in your sketchbook.

You will need to use fashion figure templates again and either layout paper or pages in your sketchbook. This time instead of using images from your research to collage on to figures you will use the photographs and drawings that you made of

drapery on the stand. Try to move the images around the figure and change the scale and placement. Repeating images on the same figure can also be successful to gain further design ideas from the initial experiments on the stand. Drawing on to the photomontage figures can add greater depth and may open up other avenues as to the eventual design outcome. You will still need to consider the same anchor points on the body for this technique.

Both techniques of collaging the research directly and working with photographs of draped stand work can then be worked further into early design ideas by redrawing and refining the garments developed in this way using layout paper or sketchbook pages.

You should now be well underway with your first design ideas and successfully bridging the gap between the research process and the design process.

<u>1</u>

Example of collaged design illustration.

<u>2</u>

Student sketchbooks exploring design drawing from photographs of modelled stand work.

2

Design development elements

*'The principle of fashion
is the principle of the
kaleidoscope. A New
Year can only bring us
a new combination of
the same elements; and
about once in so often
we go back and begin
again.'*

Katherine F. Gerould,
National Geographic
Fashion, Cathy Newman

As already discussed, research is guided through a set of required elements or components, which you must consider and gather information for; components such as shape and structure, texture and colour, and historical influences, for example.

It is these elements that now become essential in developing your ideas into garment shapes and details, determining fabric qualities, the use of colour and print, and ultimately the creative direction that the collection is going to take.

There is a process for design and perhaps even an order that you should begin to consider the following elements in. By exploring all of them you will achieve a greater and more in-depth understanding of your collection and the concept you have developed.

Design elements

- Silhouette
- Proportion and line
- Function
- Details
- Colour
- Fabric
- Print and embellishment
- Historic references
- Contemporary trends
- Market, levels and genres in fashion

Silhouette

The silhouette of a garment is often the first thing that the viewer will see and respond to when the garment is presented down the catwalk. Silhouette simply means the outline or shape that is cast around the body by a garment. It is something that is essential to the development of a collection and seen from a distance before the details, fabric or texture can be discerned.

Closely allied with silhouette is volume. The fullness, bulk or lack of it is readily seen in a garment style and its silhouette. A garment can also contain qualities of lightness or weight through the use of padded, heavy or sheer fabrics, which will again affect the silhouette that is achieved.

When designing the silhouette try to consider the garment from all angles, 360 degrees, as the silhouette may not be obvious from the first front-view impression.

Developing and refining a silhouette is important to the whole process of design as it will unify and help create an identity for your collection. Inspiration for the silhouette should come from the different elements of your research, specifically shapes and structures or perhaps from historical dress. Looking at abstract shapes in your research and then applying them to a figure is the first stage of basic design development.

1

Balenciaga A/W07. Designed by Nicolas Ghesquiere. The use of a wide belt and black panels in the sleeve and body of the jacket create an illusion of an hourglass silhouette. Catwalking.com.

Historical silhouettes

There have been many notable and often dramatic silhouettes in historical dress that have given an insight into the changes in what was seen as the desirable body shape of the time. During the 18th century the fashion was to accentuate the hourglass form of the body to its most extreme through the use of corsets, enormous powdered wigs and huge crinolines. Women's French court dress and the earliest known dressmaker, Rose Bertin, and her patron Marie Antoinette epitomised this fashion. During the late 19th century the Victorians picked up on this silhouette once again, using corsets and huge padded crinolines to increase the scale of the skirt and accentuate the tiny waist.

Christian Dior shocked the world after the Second World War with his New Look in 1947. The collection reintroduced the nipped in waist and gathered full skirt, and used much more luxurious fabrics and was a move away from the more austere fashions of the war period and the rationing it brought. The second half of the 20th century brought hem lines up and exposing legs became much more acceptable; 1960s' designer, Mary Quant, created the mini skirt and as they had in the 1920s, women subverted the fashion for the hourglass silhouette and wore their hair short and flattened their busts.

More recently, designers such as Viktor & Rolf, Comme des Garçon and Gareth Pugh have played with the use of scale and proportion in the silhouettes that they have created, often moving away from traditional aesthetics of the body's shape. Their work can be linked more closely with sculptural even architectural forms.

1
Viktor & Rolf A/W03. In this collection, Viktor & Rolf explore the idea of scale, proportion and repetition in its design detailing. Catwalking.com.

2
Jonathan Saunders A/W07. These examples show how the use of colour can divide the body into different shapes and proportions. Here we see the H, the hourglass and the empire line. Catwalking.com.

1

Proportion and line

The proportion of a garment refers to how the body is divided up either through lines – horizontal, vertical or curved – or through the use of blocks of colour or texture and fabric. The combination of these elements can create infinite and diverse possibilities.

The proportions of the body can be seen through the changes in waist, hem, and necklines and are often judged by the client on their own personal view of their bodies and what suits their body shape.

The line of a garment generally relates to its cut and the placement of seams and darts. These can create visually interesting effects, such as lengthening the body or giving the illusion of a narrower waist. The empire line from the late-18th century raised the waistline under the bust and gave the illusion of a lengthened body.

General rules:

1. Vertical lines tend to lengthen the body.
2. Horizontal lines widen the body.
3. Curved lines or lines cut on the bias will create a more curvaceous and feminine look.
4. Straight lines tend to be seen as more masculine and structured.
5. Seams and darts are not standard and can be moved around the body.

Bias cut: This is when you cut or drape a fabric on a 45-degree angle to the selvage or the horizontal or vertical woven threads called the straight of grain.

Function

The function of a garment refers to what it is: A dress, a skirt, trousers or perhaps a jacket. The brief you are working towards will often give you guidelines as to what is expected at the end of the design process, so it is important that you are clear on what types of garments you are designing.

Function can also relate to garments that have a purpose and specific demands, for example, garments for the sportswear industry will need to consider performance, fabric qualities and the type of sport they are to be worn for. It is important at the design stage to know what types of garments you are designing and what purpose they need to serve.

1
Vivienne Westwood menswear jacket. The vest-styled jacket is given a new twist and function with the detail and cut of an armour-inspired sleeve.

2
Christopher Kane S/S07. The designer has focused a strong detail on the bust using ring fastenings and stretch lace as the emphasis. Catwalking.com.

1

Details

A garment can have a wonderful silhouette and good line, but it will be the details that define and differentiate it from other designers' work. The details are what will often clinch a sale. As the client inspects the garment more closely they are able to see more than just the shape and cut, such as interesting fastenings, topstitching, unusual pockets, collar styles and belts. These are all elements to be considered in the design process and will allow you to explore more subtle changes and developments in similar garments in your collection.

The use of clever detailing is often seen and used more widely in menswear, as extreme silhouettes and bold fabrics are less likely to be used to create new and inventive designs for a largely conservative clientele.

An exercise you could do to explore this idea of detailing is to start by drawing out six of the same basic shirt shapes. Then explore the possibilities of different detailing and design six different shirts.

Details to consider:

- Topstitching and different methods of stitching
- Fastenings, zips, buttons, hook and eye, eyelets, lace up, straps, Velcro, poppers
- Collar, lapel and cuff styles
- Yoke shapes
- Sleeve shapes
- Dress straps and necklines
- Pocket styles
- Belts
- Finishing of seams, bound, French, channel

Colour

Colour is a fundamental consideration in the design process. It is often the first element that is noticed about a design and influences how that garment or collection is perceived. Colour can often be the starting point of a collection and the design process. Choosing colours, or a palette for a collection is one of the earliest decisions that you must make as it will often dictate the mood or season you are working towards. It is therefore vital that you have a basic understanding of colour theory and how colour can be created and coordinated.

The colour wheel is an exercise you can try yourself and will help you understand the basics of mixing colour; you will need to have tubes of either watercolour or gouache paint, water, palette and a fine paintbrush.

Although it is important to understand colour most designers will not choose their colour palettes or schemes based on theories.

Having got to grips with basic colour theory and mixing colour it will be important to reflect on the original sources of inspiration for the direction you take your colour palette in. It may well be that you explore a variety of ideas using different colour combinations before focusing on one group to design with.

There are 12 segments of the colour wheel starting with:

Primary colours
Red, yellow and blue cannot be made by mixing other colours.

Secondary colours
Orange, green and violet are created by mixing two of the primary colours together.

Tertiary colours
Red-orange, orange-yellow, green-yellow, blue-green, violet-blue and red-violet.

Once you have mixed these colours they will form a circle or wheel as they go around infusing with each other.

Other terminologies used to describe colour are the following:

Tint – A pure colour mixed with white, for example, red and white make pink.

Shade – A pure colour mixed with black, for example, blue and black make navy blue.

Patina – The surface texture of the described colour.

Tone – A general term to describe a tint or shade.

Hue – This describes the position of a colour on the colour wheel.

Complementary colours – These are pairs of colours that appear on opposite sides of the colour wheel, for example, red and green, blue and orange, and yellow and violet.

Analogous colours – Those colours with a common hue that are adjacent on the colour wheel, for example, blue-violet, violet and red-violet.

1
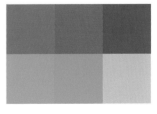
2

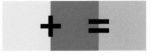

1

Examples of primary and
secondary colours.

2

An example of an analogous
colour palette.

3–4

Two examples of a colour wheel.

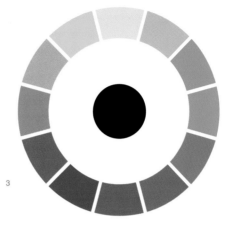

3

4

Fabric

The selection of fabric for a garment is often essential to its success. It is both the visual and sensual element of fashion design. The weight and handle of a fabric will determine the way a garment hangs and falls on the body. Designers will often select fabric before designing a garment, gaining inspiration from the way it looks, feels and handles. As already discussed it may well be that you have sourced interesting textures and swatches of cloth during the research stage and can now start to use them in the development of a collection or garment.

It is important to note that the silhouette is often affected by the quality or fabric that is used, for example, a silk jersey will naturally drape and flow around the body, where as a heavier wool will have more structure and create more volume and shape.

Fabric selection is also about function and performance, in other words, is it fit for the purpose required? For example, denim fabric is used in jeans and workwear because of its hardwearing qualities, whilst Teflon-coated cotton is often used in rainproof sportswear clothing.

Fabrics will often influence the season that is being designed for as heavier weight fabrics tend to be used in the autumn/winter and lighter weights in the spring/summer.

They are also selected for their aesthetic qualities, in other words how they look, feel and support the creative direction you have chosen, whether it be through print, texture or embellishment.

When you start to use fabric in the design process it is important to source different qualities, weights and types so that you are not limited in the garments you design. Remember that a collection should have variety and depth and should not simply be about dresses or skirts.

1
Sarah Arnett-designed silk jersey dress demonstrating the fluidity of the fabric when draped on the body.

2
Basso & Brooke S/S07. Digitally printed kimono-inspired embroidered cape.

3
Sarah Arnett A/W07. Digitally printed dress inspired by constructivist and art deco graphics, mixed with natural forms.

2

3

Print and embellishment

Print is a fundamental consideration in the design of a single garment or in the development of a whole collection. The print will often illustrate the colour palette, themes and influences the designer has been exposed to. Consider a collection inspired by constructivist art and art deco patterns and how these would inform colour and pattern in the garments designed.

Print can be something that is all over the garment in a repeat, it can be a motif in a more considered placement on the garment or it can be engineered to fit the pattern pieces of the garment. New technologies in digital printing have allowed designers such as Basso & Brooke, Ashish and Sarah Arnett to fully exploit digital print in their collections and actually feature it as their individual selling point, a factor you may wish to consider if you are going to stand out in the industry.

We have already discussed the different types of fabric embellishment in chapter one, such as appliqué, smocking, beading and embroidery. The benefits of embellishment are that they give a more three-dimensional and decorative effect to the fabric, and can also help shape or create volume in the garment. The research you have gathered will perhaps have explored the potential of such techniques in the sources of inspiration, for example, early 18th-century smocking and embroidery details, or African bead work.

It is now time to develop ideas through the use of these techniques in your design work and through careful consideration of scale, placement and choice of technique, you can start to add greater depth and invention to your garments.

Bridging the gap > **Design development elements** > Ideas generating exercise

Historic references

With so much dress history to look at it is no surprise that many designers will look to the past or to other cultures for inspiration. We have already discussed the importance of having an awareness of dress history and how it can provide valuable insight and design details for you to apply to your own creative ideas.

Using the information gathered in the research related to historical dress or even perhaps vintage clothing you can now begin to analyse the elements of design that can be gained from this source, for example, looking at historical silhouettes, construction details, proportion and line, fabric, print and embellishments. You should now be considering all of these design elements in the design of a garment and a collection can be explored from the historical content of your research.

Vivienne Westwood has in many of her collections used direct references to historical silhouettes, garment styles and prints, famously those based on the archives of The Wallace Collection and on the French 18th-century aristocracy. She has also drawn inspiration from paintings of period dress, referring to the artist Watteau and the women he painted as a source of inspiration.

A warning should perhaps be given that whilst it is important to look at historical and cultural dress and costume it should not be simply recreated, as this starts to move more into the area of costume design and not fashion. Remember it is about selecting elements of the period source or country of origin and synthesising them into something new, perhaps by mixing with other references from your research or altering the proportions, the placement, the use of fabric or even the gender the garment is aimed at.

1
Watteau evening dress by Vivienne Westwood, UK, 1996. Watteau-inspired couture dress. V&A Images/Victoria and Albert Museum.

2
Bora Aksu S/S07. Converse trainer-inspired corset top.

3
Classic converse canvas hi-top trainer. A staple item found in streetwear fashion.

> *'Show me the clothes of a country and I can write its history.'*
>
> Anatole France, National Geographic Fashion, Cathy Newman

Contemporary trends

'The fashionable woman wears clothes. The clothes don't wear her.'

Mary Quant

We have looked at the importance of contemporary trends, through forecasting agencies, global and social interests and even the 'bubble-up' effect from street cultures.

The research you have gathered may well contain some of this type of information and as a designer it is important to have an awareness of

what is going on around you and how it may affect your designs and ultimately the client you are creating the garments for. Using some of the trend information within your design work may well provide useful starting points for some of the design elements, such as colour, fabric or function.

2

3

Market, levels and genres of fashion

As a fashion designer it will be essential for you to consider the market that you are designing for and where you see yourself in what is a very diverse and broad-ranging industry. Finding your niche or level will be an important development in your growth as a designer. Therefore you should understand the different market levels and genres in order that you can be a more successful designer.

There are essentially two main approaches to garment design and production, haute couture (French for 'high dressmaking') and prêt-à-porter (French for 'ready to wear'). But as with all industries these approaches have subdivided over the years into a further series of levels that are more specialist and focused on specific target markets.

Haute couture

Couture is the oldest form of designing and making clothes and was and still is exclusive to Paris, France. The couture fashion shows are held twice a year in Paris, once in January and then again in July. They showcase to the buyers, specially invited clientele and press the absolute top-end, one-off, most expensive, and often most creative and innovative designs that the couture houses have produced.

The industry supports a wealth of amazingly talented and skilled craftspeople from lace makers, beading and embroidery specialists to highly skilled pattern cutters and seamstresses. Some of the most well-known design houses that still produce couture are Christian Dior, Givenchy, Christian Lacroix, Jean Paul Gaultier, Yves Saint Laurent and Versace.

2

<u>1</u>
Balenciaga prêt-à-porter S/S07.
Designer Nicolas Ghesquiere.
Catwalking.com.

<u>2</u>
Christian Dior haute couture
S/S07. Designer John Galliano.

Although there are now very few people across the world who are able to afford haute couture, it still plays a vital role in the industry as it has few constraints on cost and creativity, and is often where ideas and aspirational ideals are first seen before they trickle down into the prêt-à-porter collections.

Ready to wear/Prêt-à-porter
The majority of the fashion buying public cannot afford couture and so the industry has developed a level of fashion called 'ready to wear'. The clothes are still made to a very high standard, but to a set of uniform sizes in much greater quantities. There is still a strong sense of design and innovation, as well as the use of beautiful fabrics and details. There are many more companies working, designing and showing collections all over the world at this level of the industry and, unlike couture, there are more opportunities to show your collections as the ready-to-wear shows are held twice a year in the different fashion capitals of the world, such as Milan, London, New York, Rio, Tokyo and of course Paris.

Luxury super brands
The luxury super brands are the giant global companies who have huge advertising budgets and are often part of a larger corporation that promotes and designs a wide variety of products throughout their own stores, such as cosmetics, perfumes, accessories and furnishings. The ready-to-wear collections that they show are merely a starting point for the vast sales on additional products that they produce.

The two main contenders in the super brand level are LVMH (Louis Vuitton Moët Hennessy) and the Gucci Group, who between them own such designer brands as Dior, Celine, Givenchy, Kenzo, Alexander McQueen, Stella McCartney, Marc Jacobs, Balenciaga, Bottega Veneta, Donna Karan, Louis Vuitton and Gucci to name but a few.

Mid-level brands and designers
A mid-level brand or designer is an established company with good sales and high profile, but without the power of the super brands. These brands are often sold through independent design stores or boutiques, department stores and franchises around the world and they may have their own stores as well. The mid-level designer will generally have a catwalk show and use this to promote a collection to buyers and the press. It is now also the trend for this level of designer to work with high street brands to create more exclusive ranges based on their own collections, for example, Julien Macdonald, Matthew Williamson and John Rocha.

Independent designer labels
The independent designer works with a small team of people to produce a collection. They have total control over the design, sampling, production, promotion and sales. The size of the business will determine how many of these tasks need to be dealt with inhouse. The independent designer label will sell wholesale to independent boutiques and department stores and will show through trade fairs and possibly through catwalk shows. Sarah Arnett shows in Paris and sells through Liberty of London.

1

Genres of fashion

There are three genres of fashion that you need to consider as a designer:

1. Womenswear
2. Menswear
3. Childrenswear

'Men's fashions start as sports clothes and progress to great occasions of state. The tailcoat, which started as a hunting coat, is finishing such a journey. The tracksuit is just beginning one.'

Angus McGill, National Geographic Fashion, Cathy Newman

Womenswear

The womenswear market is the most diverse and directional, as women will purchase clothing much more so than men in any one season. Womenswear allows you to be more creative with styles and fabrics and it is seen to be more glamorous. Because of this it is rather overly populated with designers and super brands, and so can be much more difficult to make your own niche or client base within it as a designer. But because of the variety and vast market you are more likely to find employment.

Menswear

This market tends to be more conservative and although there are seasonal ranges the changes tend to be subtler. Men generally don't buy in to as many fashion fads as women and tend to have more classic pieces in their wardrobes. As a result of this, sales in this genre are less than in womenswear.

Childrenswear

Childrenswear design can be just as interesting as the other two genres and often it will follow similar trends to the main lines. Design brands such as Christian Dior and Versace all do lines in childrenswear. There tend to be more constraints than in the other genres, such as health and safety, durability and function, as in the case of newborn children and toddlers.

Casualwear and sportswear brands

Just as with the ready-to-wear designer market there are super brands within the more focused fashion design industry surrounding sportswear and casualwear, such as Nike, Reebok and Levi Strauss.

Just as with the super brands these niche brands can control a vast global market and can actually influence and impact every walk of life. The Nike logo has become one of the most recognised symbols in the world and is not only related to sportswear, but also to a lifestyle. There are also mid-level design brands such as Diesel, Evisu, and G-Star.

High street

The high street has become one of the fastest growing and most diverse marketplaces in fashion design. Companies are able to react quickly to trends on the catwalk because of the way their design, manufacturing and quality development is set up. Because of the quantities they produce, they can sell at much cheaper prices than designer brands.

The high street in the UK is one of the most directional in the world and stores like Topshop and H&M are fast becoming the favourite places for even the rich and famous to shop at. Equally, places such as Debenhams, which is a large high street retail store, is employing designers like Julien Macdonald and Matthew Williamson to produce exclusive ranges for them and in doing so offer that designer's brand name without the designer price tag.

Ideas generating exercise

You have already been shown how to literally translate elements of your research on to figures to help with the early brainstorming of ideas. What this exercise now shows you is how to get the most from these collaged figures and how to begin the process of design development, or collection development.

The collaged figures you produced in the earlier exercise will have developed ideas mainly for shape and perhaps quite abstract shapes on the body were explored. What now needs to be considered is how through the addition of these other elements a series of related ideas can be developed from just a few initial collages.

You need to think of design development as being like a family tree, all the ideas start from just a handful of key ideas and through the addition and mixing of other references and from playing with the design elements, such as proportion and line, fabric, print and function, a collection that has similarities yet differences can be generated.

Take three collages from the early brainstorming exercise on figures (they are labelled A, B, C for this explanation):

A   B   C

Take each collage and design three variations of that collage, perhaps add colour and indicate a print, change a neckline, add a pocket, change the function or type of garment. This will then give you three groups of ideas:

(Ax3)   (Bx3)   (Cx3)

Then from these new ideas that have similar qualities start to mix across and see how the best elements from each grouping can affect the other:

(ABx3)   (BCx3)

And then mix once more:

(ABCx3)

So from the initial three collaged figures, you have now drawn up 18 further design ideas and all of them
will have a relationship or similarity to each other. This is essentially what design development or collection development is about. Taking a set of known design elements and mixing them up to create a series or collection of garments.

Design development elements > Ideas generating exercise > Development and refinement of individual garments

Development and refinement of individual garments

Now that the basic understanding of design development has been explained it is important for you to refine and develop more specific garments from the early experiments that you have drawn.

The collages and family tree ideas will have begun to explore different combinations of the design elements and hopefully provided you with a set of initial designs.

You may well have established a strong silhouette or line in some of your work, or perhaps the use of a colour palette or prints was key to their appeal? It is these components that will remain the constant while you develop and further refine the collection.

What this next stage will achieve is to separate out the different types of garments – such as jackets and tailoring, knitwear and jersey, dresses, skirts, trousers, blouses and shirts and outerwear – and begin to focus on the design of variations on these specific types, as a strong collection should contain all of these.

A designer will often have a silhouette and colour palette that is consistent throughout the collection, but by changes in garment type, fabric, use of print and subtle changes to details, he or she is able to create many more outfits in the range.

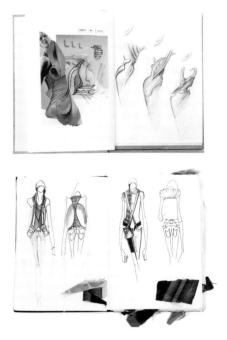

Design exercise:

Identify one garment type from the drawings you have already produced, perhaps a dress. Take this garment and start to design as many variations as you can again using the design elements to help you with the development process. Consider changing necklines, hemlines, sleeves, collars, cuffs, fastenings, stitching, use of fabric, pockets, proportions and line, embellishments and possible use of print, but remember to stay true to the original idea, this may well have been the silhouette that was created on the body in the initial collages. You should be able to come up with ten or 20 variations on this one garment and if you then apply this method to all the other garment types you can easily create a set of design developments into the hundreds.

Ideas generating exercise > **Development and refinement of individual garments** > Selecting and editing your ideas to form a collection

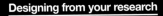

Selecting and editing your ideas to form a collection

<u>1–2</u>
Examples of final design edit and selection process.

<u>3</u>
Collaged fashion design line up.

By this stage you should now have a clear vision throughout your designs. The key elements that you have worked with should be apparent and fully explored. Colour, print and fabrics will all have been indicated and considered throughout the process of development and refinement, as well as styles and types of garment.

A good designer will produce hundreds of design sketches, with many variations and subtle detail changes and will then have the task of selecting the strongest ideas to take forward into the final collection edit. It is this stage of the development process that is crucial to the overall success of a collection, as you will need to edit back your designs to create a coherent, well balanced and harmonious collection.

The first thing to identify is the key pieces or your favourite elements of the collection: for example, dresses, tailoring, jersey or knitwear, skirts, shorts, trousers, jackets, outerwear. Initially you should try to build on one piece for each of these types, although it may depend on the season as to the types of garments that are expected in the collection. You generally don't see swimwear in autumn/ winter collections.

From these key pieces you will need to add in any other important design ideas, for instance the same jacket or dress, but created in several different fabrics. Print often plays a key role in the unifying of a collection and is generally seen in several incarnations, a dress, a skirt or a blouse. The portrayal of a silhouette, as we have already discussed, is also key to the harmony of a collection and can be seen in many different garments, as can the details that may be placed on them. All these elements will create running themes in the final edit and help to establish the final look of the collection.

So how many pieces or outfits should be in a collection? This really depends on the size of the design company or the budget, as the next stage of the process is pattern cutting, sampling and manufacturing and an independent label may only have the resources to create 20 outfits in any one season, whereas Gucci or Christian Dior may have well over 80–100 outfits in their catwalk presentations as they have the money and manufacturing to support this number. As an aspiring new designer and more often in the academic forum you will probably be working towards collections of between eight to ten outfits.

1

2

'In difficult times fashion is always outrageous.'

Elsa Schiaparelli

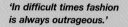

3

'Fashion illustration is one art form interpreted by another.'

David Downton, fashion illustrator

The ability to communicate your ideas is an essential part of
being a fashion designer, getting what is in your head on to
paper. In this chapter we will discuss the various approaches
to rendering your ideas and designs, exploring different
methods and use of mixed media. Art materials are
explained as well as how they can be used to illustrate
different fabric qualities.

Design sketching is only one aspect of fashion drawing and
the chapter also analyses the function of working drawings
and the use of templates. Finally fashion illustration and the
role it plays in the industry are explored, and there is an
interview with the world-renowned illustrator David Downton

Sketching and design drawing

> **'I don't design clothes.
> I design dreams.'**
>
> Ralph Lauren

The ability to communicate your thoughts and designs is an essential part of being a fashion designer. Not only is it a part of the development process, but also a way of explaining your thoughts to others. Although it is an important part of the design process, you do not have to be an excellent illustrator or draughtsperson, or even be good at drawing, but it does obviously help.

Having a good understanding of the human anatomy, for example, muscular shapes, proportion, balance, stance and skeletal structure, will assist in the ability to draw and ultimately design more convincingly. One way you can develop this skill is to attend life-drawing classes, which are often available as evening classes at your local college or adult education centre.

Another approach to developing your drawing is to sketch people on the move, perhaps walking past a café, on the subway or in the street. Capturing people in motion and seeing how their clothes move and respond to the body is also an important part of understanding how fashion can be drawn.

In academic schools, fashion drawing and sketching is often given a lot of time and attention as the ability to visually describe your designs and develop them through drawing with originality and personality is one of the fundamental parts of the design process.

1
Example of design sketching.

2
Design sketching incorporating colour and further details of construction.

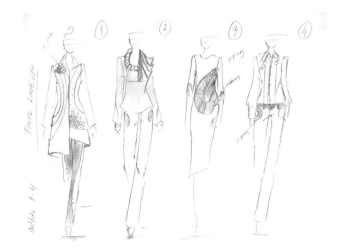

The design sketch must be figurative, in other words vaguely resemble the human form, although it can be stylised and stretched, long legs are an aesthetic to consider, as models on the catwalk tend to have long legs.

The sketch needs to describe the key design elements, in other words, it is important to draw not only the silhouette, but also the garment details, fabrics selected, print ideas and colours used. It is the main tool used in exploring ideas; rendering the figure many times over will allow you to play with the design elements in different combinations.

The design sketch itself should be something that is quick and allows you to get your ideas down rapidly. The mind can move very quickly and wander off into different directions as you get more inspired by the research you have gathered. Speed often provides spontaneity and energy to your design work. Mastering your own style will also present uniqueness to your designs and add to the identity of the work.

Having the basic skills in figure drawing and mark-making will always assist in the speed and accuracy of your rendered design work, but one tool that can help with this process is a fashion template.

Mark-making

Mark-making is the name given to the practice of using different art media and the methods of putting marks on to paper in a creative and expressionistic way (see pages 154–155).

Sketching and design drawing > Templates

Templates

Fashion templates are pre-drawn figures that can be used by tracing them off through layout paper or trace paper and then drawing designs over the top. Templates allow you to focus on the design work and not on the figure. They also allow you to work quickly and in a more repetitive manner, perhaps working on the same type of garment many times until the strongest design appears.

Templates can be found in most illustration fashion books, but where possible it is best to try and develop your own figures to work on, as they will be more individual and help you develop your own style and hand in fashion figure drawing.

The example here shows the development of a fashion figure through the different stages of development, from initially mapping out the proportions of the head, shoulders, waist and legs to marking in the figure, then the garment shapes and details and eventually the colour and texture of the fabrics.

1

In these examples you can see how a basic design template is developed through a series of stages considering proportion, balance, garment shape, colour and fabric rendering.

Collage

1–2
Student examples demonstrating the use of collage on figures for illustration and design.

3
Research is collaged on to the figure to create a more atmospheric and evocative illustration.

We have already discussed the approaches of using collage in both your research and early design work, but collage can also be a vital tool in the rendering and illustration of your fashion designs. Working with not only components of your research, but also a variety of mixed media and different paper qualities can provide a very effective and original looking design sketch.

The use of collage will also provide a freer and sometimes more expressive approach to the design process. Collage is best used alongside drawing at this stage, as the details of the garments designed can be lost in the use of large pieces of photographic, perhaps more impressionistic, images.

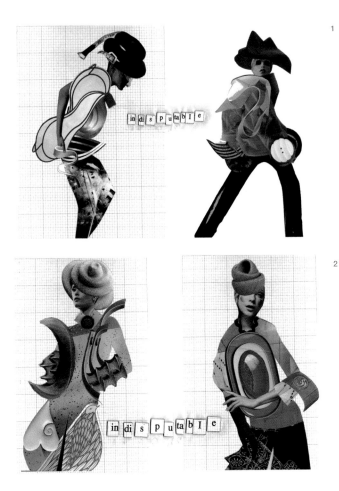

1

2

Working drawings

Final portfolio working drawing and technical specification sheets. Here you can see that each garment is clearly represented with both front and back details drawn.

Working drawings, specs, flats or technical drawings, as they are often referred to, are the diagrammatical detailed drawings of your design work. They are the graphic, clearly drawn explanation of the garment, showing all the construction details, such as seams, darts, pockets, fastenings and topstitching.

The flats are drawn with no figure represented, but to scale and as the name suggests in a flat rendering, with no indication of colour, texture or form. They will also show both the front and the back of the garment, something that is often forgotten in the design sketch.

The working drawing is used to support the sometimes more fluid and artistic design sketch and must always be presented with the correct body proportions, as it is generally the drawing that a pattern cutter will interpret a pattern from, as the design sketch can sometimes lead to inaccurate proportions.

A working drawing is generally produced using either fine liner black pens or a clutch pencil, which uses fine leads. Different widths of fine liner can be used in the same drawing to illustrate different components, for example, a 0.8mm thick pen can be used for all the seam lines, darts and details, where as a 0.3mm thick pen can then be used to indicate all the topstitching, buttons and fastenings.

Flats

CUAD.fig.007 (a.)

Grey and black lambs wool striped jumper with fairisle 'fence' pattern and uneven spacing with grey suede hood and sleeves that have been etched with the same fence graphic.

CUAD.fig.007 (b.)

Black discharge printed trousers with extreme drop crotch and tight fitting spat around the foot and ankle.

CUAD.fig.008 (c.)

Circular jacket in beige suiting with a shawl collar, taped seam details and hidden side pockets with draped fullness around the hips

CUAD.fig.008 (d.)

Grey high waisted trousers in cashmere suiting with d-ring tie details in pockets and below knees so that trousers may be worn in several ways.

Flats

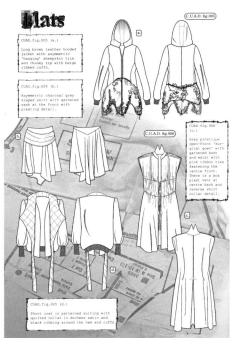

CUAD.fig.005 (a.)

Long brown leather hooded jacket with asymmetric 'hanging' sheepskin trim and chunky zip with beige ribbed cuffs.

CUAD.fig.005 (b.)

Asymmetric charcoal grey draped skirt with gathered sash at the front with pleating detail.

CUAD.fig.006 (c.)

Grey pinstripe open-front 'surgical gown' with gathered bust and waist with pink ribbon ties fastening the centre front. There is a box pleat vent at centre back and reverse shirt collar detail.

CUAD.fig.005 (d.)

Short coat in patterned suiting with quilted collar in duchess satin and black ribbing around the hem and cuffs.

Flats

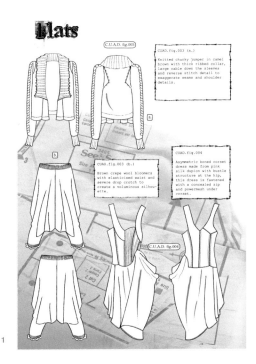

CUAD.fig.003 (a.)

Knitted chunky jumper in camel brown with thick ribbed collar, large cable down the sleeves and reverse stitch detail to exaggerate seams and shoulder details.

CUAD.fig.003 (b.)

Brown crepe wool bloomers with elasticised waist and severe drop crotch to create a voluminous silhouette.

CUAD.fig.004

Asymmetric boned corset dress made from pink silk dupion with bustle structure at the hip, this dress is fastened with a concealed zip and powermesh under corset.

Flats

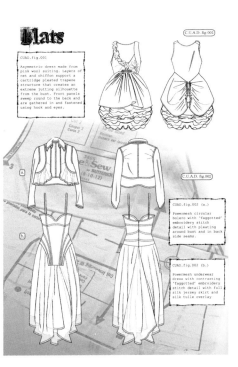

CUAD.fig.001

Asymmetric dress made from pink wool suiting. Layers of net and chiffon support a cartridge pleated trapeze structure that creates an extreme jutting silhouette from the bust. Front panels sweep round to the back and are gathered in and fastened using hook and eyes.

CUAD.fig.002 (a.)

Powermesh circular bolero with 'faggotted' embroidery stitch detail with pleating around bust and in back side seams.

CUAD.fig.002 (b.)

Powermesh underwear dress with contrasting 'faggotted' embroidery stitch detail with full silk jersey skirt and silk tulle overlay

Collage > Working drawings > Art materials

1

Art materials

1. Adhesive glue stick
2. Acrylic paint
3. Gouache paint
4. Watercolour paint
5. Water-soluble colouring pencils
6. Paintbrushes
7. Magic marker or brush pen
8. Fine-line pen
9–10. Clutch pencil and lead
11. Putty rubber
12. Pencil sharpener
13. Layout paper

The use of a variety of art materials is important throughout the whole process of research and design as it allows you to explore your own hand and preferred media. It also allows you to illustrate a variety of images and interpret them into new forms, patterns, colours and textures. It is therefore essential that you equip yourself with the basics and understand how they can be used. Illustrated here are a few of the basics you should become familiar with.

1   2   3   4

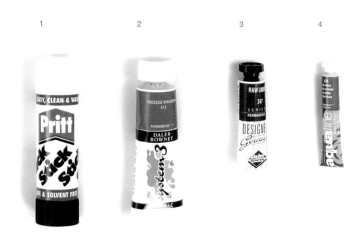

5

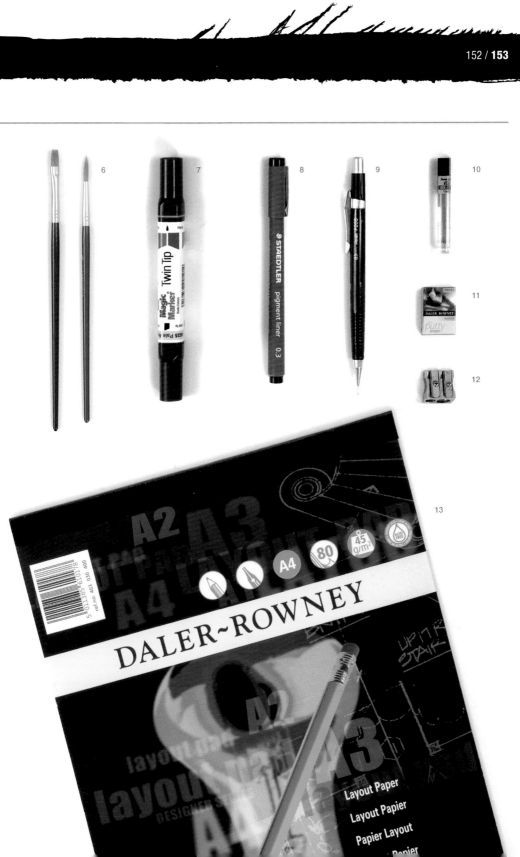

1

<u>1</u>

An illustration by Linda Ramstedt demonstrating the use of mixed media to achieve the appearance of woven fabric in the design illustration.

<u>2</u>

Fabric and illustration board. Here you can see several examples of how different fabrics can be rendered through the use of mixed media.

On the pervious page you have been shown a variety of art equipment. Here are some explanations and possible uses for them:

1. Adhesive glue stick

Glue sticks or Pritt stick is dry glue that is particularly useful for sticking paper, as it does not soak through as PVA glue can. This glue is essential when using collage in your research and also in the experimental design stages. It does not dry immediately on contact and so allows you to reposition images when necessary.

2. Acrylic paint

Acrylic paint is a water-based paint. It will dry with the textures and brush marks created through application. It can have a slightly glossy look and can be used to render plastic and leather garments successfully.

3. Gouache paint

Unlike acrylic paint gouache will dry flat and even with an opaque finish. It is slightly matt and chalky in finish and allows you to either water it down to get a lighter shade or use more thickly to get a darker shade. It is a good paint to block in even colour and can be used with other media, such as oil pastels and coloured pencils to render different textures and fabric qualities.

4. Watercolour paint

This is a transparent paint that is used with water, as its name suggests. It can be bought in tubes or in solid blocks that can be purchased as sets. It will mix well and will take on the characteristics of the paper it is painted on, in other words, used on coloured paper it will take on the colour of that paper, as a tint. It is great for illustrating more sheer and delicate fabrics because of its transparent

qualities. Used with plenty of water it will dilute to very pale and subtle shades. It works best on a good quality cartridge or watercolour paper.

5. Water-soluble colouring pencils

These are a quick and easy way to apply and mix colour directly on to your drawings. Used dry they can give the impression of texture and the weave of a fabric, while used with a little water, applied with a brush, they can be mixed to present a more transparent fluid mark.

6. Paintbrushes

Always invest in a good set of brushes in a variety of widths made from natural fibres, such as sable. They will last longer and will not flare after use, which can make accurate painting difficult. Both flat and round heads are useful, as they will allow you to make different types of brush marks and illustrate different details. Always wash your brushes thoroughly after use and remove all residue paint or ink.

7. Magic marker or brush pen

These are superior felt tip pens and come in a huge variety of colours and shades that will often allow you to match up exactly to your colour palette.

They will lay down colour evenly and flat and also allow you to build up layers and darker tones.

They can be expensive but are well worth the expense as they are the quickest and simplest way to put colour accurately into a design sketch.

Marker pens can also be used with other media such as coloured pencils and can often be the base colour to a fabric with the pencils providing the texture.

8. Fine-line pen

The fine-line pen comes in a variety of thicknesses and is generally used in the rendering of designs and particularly working drawings, as it gives a precise, graphic and even mark.

9–10. Clutch pencil and lead

The clutch pencil is a reusable pencil that can have the lead replaced and changed, as it is needed. You can vary the grade, from hard 4H, to soft 3B, depending on your requirements. For design sketching it is best to have a lead that is anywhere from B to 3B and in the pattern cutting room it is better to have a harder lead, H to 3H. The benefits, apart from the ability to change the grade, are that you always have a sharp, precise mark, which is essential in design work.

11. Putty rubber

This is a more mouldable rubber than normal hard erasers. It can therefore be more precise for removing pencil marks and smudges.

12. Pencil sharpener

This is used to sharpen normal pencils and watercolour pencils to achieve a clean, sharp mark on the page.

13. Layout paper

This is a slightly transparent lightweight paper that is used in the design drawing process. It is perfect for using with templates as they can just be seen through the paper and therefore allow you to trace the figure quickly and easily before applying the design work.

You can purchase different types of layout pads, particularly ones that work with magic markers as they stop the bleeding through to other pages. Because the paper is lightweight it is not recommended that you use any wet media with it, as it will tend to buckle and disintegrate.

The picture below shows a variety of fabrics that have been rendered using many of the art materials described. Note the use of mixed media in many cases to achieve the results successfully.

2

Sheep Skin

woven check

Beaded Lace

Dogtooth check

Harris Tweed check

Silk Brocade

Layout and composition

The layout and composition of your work will greatly depend on how you have presented your designs. Most of the work you do will be contained in a sketchbook or on sheets of layout paper, these can then be bound into one presentation. The layout of a design page will often require you to work on figures in a series of groups – three as a minimum and up to six – in a row across the page and generally on A3-sized paper.

This allows you to develop ideas across several figures at the same time and see immediately any connections, running themes or similarities in design. The layout therefore becomes much more simplistic and uniformed as the design becomes more important, just rows of figures with the design applied to them.

As the design becomes more selected and refined the figures and their composition can become more complex and creative. Because the designs have been edited you are able to spend more time on the drawing and rendering of the individual figures and designs they show. There are no hard and fast rules and whether you choose to work in portrait or landscape format is really up to you.

Line-ups and groupings of the final collection can be presented in a variety of ways and they can often be influenced by the themes that have occurred throughout the research and design process. Using different positions, stances and styles of drawing, perhaps influenced by a period, for example, the 1920s' Poiret illustrations, can all have an effect on the final layout and look of the design work.

Using fashion magazines and photo shoots can often suggest the positions and groupings that could be considered in a final presentation. Figures sitting, standing next to one another, one in the distance one up close – it will really be down to your own personal preferences.

The composition and layout of these selected designs is then the final part of the process and rendering the design work and considering the format is an important part of the presentation of this work. The creativity you have developed throughout the research and design process can now be concluded in the final designs and the way you choose to show them. There are no rules, but remember, it should always be about the clothes.

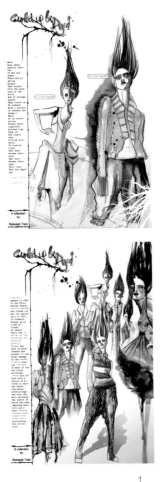

1

1–2
Student examples of final portfolio design illustration layouts.

in di s p u ta b I e

Multilayered collars on a tailored asymetric jacket.
Straight trousers with round pockets in contrast fabric

in di s p u ta b I e

1.Fitted jerseydress wih rows of piping and ribbing for effect. 3/4 lenght sleeves with pipingdetail on cuffs

Illustration

Communicating your ideas

1–2

An example of David Downton's fashion illustrations. These demonstrate more traditional painted qualities and brush mark techniques.

It is important to know the difference between fashion design sketching and illustration, as the two play quite different roles. As discussed earlier in the book, the design sketches are about the clothes, they show the silhouette, details, fabrics, print, embellishments and colour. They are used to describe and show the clothing, as it would be worn, they are generally in proportion and they represent a visual tool to help the pattern cutter create the garment. They are also quick and can appear more spontaneous.

Illustration, on the other hand, is seen as an art form in itself, as it allows you to be even more creative with your use of media and the quality of lines or brush marks that are laid out on the paper become more important and influential on the way the garments are perceived. Illustration is about evoking the mood of the collection and need not show the garments in full or even in a way that is obvious as to what they are. The work is much more expressive and stylised and often captures the spirit or even the character or muse that the collection was created for. The wide use of mixed media, digital and Photoshop software can all be explored.

David Downton, fashion illustrator, interview   www.daviddownton.com

Here we have a brief interview with David Downton, who for years has been one of the most successful fashion illustrators in the world, and has continued to use more traditional methods in his work.

What is fashion illustration?

Fashion illustration is one art form interpreted by another, in other words, it is a designer's vision filtered through an artist's creativity. It absolutely requires you to respect the work of the designer and it should bring out the best of the both of you. When working with haute couture particularly, I am well aware of how much has gone into each of the pieces, having met many of the people involved, and I do feel a real responsibility to attempt to do it justice. I do

sometimes feel guilty using such a reductive line to describe something so intricate. Classical illustration such as this, going to view the catwalk presentations and distilling the essence of the shows through drawing, is a rarity now.

Fashion illustration has changed beyond recognition over the last decade. There are no rules, no restrictions and no prescribed way of working. There is no prevalent style and hand-drawn and digitally made imagery have an equal validity today. The market has broadened to embrace club flyers, CD covers, gallery exhibitions, as well as the more traditional outlets of newspapers and magazines. To sum up I would say there has never been a better or more confusing time to be a fashion illustrator.

1

Layout and composition > **Illustration**

To conclude, this book has presented you with an in-depth approach to researching ideas for design. We have discussed all the different sources available to you from museums and art galleries to the street and costume. The basic elements of research and design have been outlined and with practice and experimentation anything is possible.

As with all creative areas, it will take time to perfect your abilities and to discover who you are and what you are about in terms of design. All the great notable designers have had a strong personal signature to their work and this can only be found through experimentation and exploration. Do not restrict yourself and never feel you have seen and done it all. A good designer will constantly challenge him or herself and always look for the next new direction and seek out further reaching influences and sources of inspiration to stimulate their work.

There have been many designers who have pushed the boundaries over the years and forced society to reflect and review its perceptions, ideals and aesthetics related to dress. Fashion is about change and about challenging what have gone before, it is about leading and not following and so you should never feel that you couldn't achieve your goals or push your design visions into the world.

With this book I hope I have started you on a journey of discovery, interest and passion, and that the contents have provided you with the insight, skills and knowledge to pursue your dreams.

I would like to thank all the talented people who have contributed to this book and I hope you have found it as exciting and inspiring as I have to write it.

Enjoy your future career in fashion and good luck!

Glossary

rdles showcase a strong contrast of satin against pow...
...dery placements are geometric or swirling florals; often ...
... a slimming effect.

Abstract
A concept that describes an idea, feeling or quality; not reality.

Aesthetic
An object or design that depicts beauty or pleasing appearance.

Anchor Points
Points on the body that a fashion illustrator or designer will use to develop shapes or forms from, such as the neck, shoulders, bust, waist and hips.

Brief
A set of instructions directed at a designer, to outline the aims, objectives, and final outcomes.

Client-based
Describes a product to be designed for a particular company or target market.

Collection
A group of garments designed with certain features in common, such as colour or shape.

Commercial
Describes a product that is intended to be bought by the general public.

Composition
The way that visual elements along with text can be arranged on a page.

Conceptual
A vision based on ideas or principles.

Consumer Analysis
Collating information about the lifestyle of the target customer group, such as age, economic status and occupation – which helps to guide the designer in creating commercially viable products.

Consumer Behaviour
The analysis of consumer lifestyle and spending habits.

Contemporary
Existing or happening now.

Contours
The surface or shape of a garment or the body formed by its outer edge.

Critical Path
The time and process involved in creating a garment or collection, from concept to creation.

Cultural Influences
Relating to the habits, traditions and beliefs of a society; or relating to music, art, theatre, literature, etc.

Customisation
To make or change elements of a garment to individualise the look or style.

Demographics
Characteristics of a population regionally or nationally, usually in relation to their age, income and expenditure.

Disparate
Different in every way.

Drape Techniques
The way in which cloth folds or hangs as it covers the body or mannequin.

Fashion Forecasting
The process of predicting forthcoming trends.

Genres
Describes a style that involves a particular set of characteristics within a category of, for example, art, literature or music.

Haute Couture
Originally a French term, meaning high-fashion custom-fitted clothing. Literally means 'high dressmaking'.

Journals
A magazine or newspaper published about a specialist subject.

Juxtaposition
To put things which are not similar next to each other.

Research and Design

Lustre
The shiny or bright surface of a fabric.

Mainstream
Lifestyle or habits adopted by the majority.

Market
The business or trade of a particular product, associated with the sale of products.

Merchandising Department
The department responsible for allocating and arranging garments creatively, for example, in window displays.

Motif
An identifiable pattern, design or logo.

Muse
An imaginary person or icon that gives a designer ideas and helps them to focus.

Narrative
A story or a series of events.

Negative Space
The space around an object that can be used in composition to balance positive space.

Niche
A specialised product group targeting a specific area of the market.

Palette
A group of colours that sit well together.

Pantone
Internationally recognised numbered shades and colours used throughout the creative industries.

Pop Art
A type of modern art that started in the 1960s and uses images and objects from everyday life.

Punk
Culture popular among young people, especially in the late 1970s, involving opposition to authority expressed through shocking behaviour, clothes, hair and music.

Season
Described in fashion terms as spring/summer or autumn/winter, usually fashion products are designed at least one season ahead.

Sensory
Connected with the physical senses of touch, smell, taste, hearing and seeing.

Silhouette
The outline shape of a garment or collection.

Subculture
A group of people who share similar customs, tastes and ideas in, for example, music.

Surrealist/ism
A cultural movement and visual art depicting unusual happenings or events, not based on reality.

Swatches
A small piece of cloth used as an example of the colour or texture of fabric or a sample.

Target Market
The group of customers that a retailer aims to sell to.

The Bubble-up Effect
Fashion seen in street or subculture that influences designer fashion.

Viewfinder
A frame that allows you to conceal or expose part of an object or image.

Visual Language
An image created to communicate an idea using line, shape, colour, texture, pattern, scale, and/or proportion.

Zeitgeist
German expression that means 'the spirit of the times'; a general set of ideas, beliefs or theories.

Glossary

Bibliography

Baal-Teshuva J (2001)
Christo and Jeanne-Claude.
Germany: Taschen.

Beckwith C and Fisher A (2002)
African Ceremonies.
New York: Harry N Abrams, Inc.

Black S., ed. (2006)
**Fashioning Fabrics: Contemporary Textiles
in Fashion.**
London: Black Dog Publishing.

**Bloom: a horti-cultural view (February 2003)
Issue 9.**
France: United Publishers SA.

Blossfeldt K (1985)
Art Forms in the Plant World.
New York: Dover Publications Inc.

Borelli L (2004)
Fashion Illustration Next.
London: Thames & Hudson.

Brogden J (1971)
Fashion Design.
London: Studio Vista.
New York: Van Nostrand Reinhold Company.

Callaway N., ed. (1988)
Issey Miyake: Photographs by Irving Penn.
Japan: Miyake Design Studio.
New York: Callaway Editions Inc.

Charles-Roux E (2005)
The World of Coco Chanel: Friends Fashion Fame.
London: Thames & Hudson.

Cole D (2003)
1000 Patterns.
London: A & C Black Publishers Ltd.

Cosgrave B (2005)
Sample: 100 Fashion Designers, 10 Curators.
London: Phaidon Press Ltd.

Currie N (1993)
Pierre et Gilles.
France: Taschen-Verlag.

Dawber M (2005)
New Fashion Illustration.
London: BT Batsford.

Diane T and Cassidy T (2005)
Colour Forecasting.
Oxford: Blackwell Publishing.

Edmaier B (2004)
**Earthsong: Aerial photographs of our
untouched planet.**
London: Phaidon Press Ltd.

Fukai A (2002)
**Fashion: The Collection of the Kyoto Costume
Institute: A History from the 18th to the
20th Century.**
Germany: Taschen.

Gallienne A and McConnico H (2005)
Colourful World.
London: Thames & Hudson.

Golbin P, Ghesquiere N and Baron F (2006)
Balenciaga Paris.
London: Thames & Hudson.

Gooding M (2002)
Patrick Heron. (PB Ed.)
London: Phaidon Press Ltd.

Gorman P (2006)
The Look: Adventures in Rock and Pop Fashion.
London: Adelita.

Hamann H (2001)
Vertical View.
UK: teNeues Publishing Ltd.

Hecker Z et al (2001)
House of the Book.
London: Black Dog Publishing.

Hillier J (2003)
Japanese Colour Prints. (1st Ed. 1966.)
London: Phaidon Press Ltd.

Hodge B, Mears P and Sidlauskas S (2006)
**Skin + Bones: Parallel Practices in Fashion
and Architecture.**
London: Thames & Hudson.

Holborn M (1995)
Issey Miyake.
Germany: Taschen.

Itten J (1973)
The Art of Color. (1st Ed. 1966.)
New York: John Wiley & Sons, Inc.

Jenkyn Jones S (2002)
Fashion Design.
London: Laurence King Publishing.

Jiricna E (2001)
Staircases.
London: Calmann & King Ltd.

O'Neill J P., ed. (2003)
Goddess: The Classical Mode.
New York: The Metropolitan Museum of Art.

Joseph-Armstrong H (2000)
Draping for Apparel Design.
New York: Fairchild Publications, Inc.

Klanten R et al., eds. (2006)
Romantik.
Berlin: Die Gestalten Verlag.

Klanten R et al., eds. (2006)
Wonderland. (2nd Ed.)
Berlin: Die Gestalten Verlag.

Bibliography

Knight N and Knapp S (2001)
Flora.
New York: Harry N. Abrams, Inc.

Koda H (2001)
Extreme Beauty: The Body Transformed.
New York: The Metropolitan Museum of Art.

Lauer D (1979)
Design Basics.
Holt, Rinehart and Winston.

Lawson B (1990)
**How Designers Think: The Design Process
Demystified.** (2nd Ed.)
Cambridge: The University Press.

Levi-Strauss C, Fukai A and Bloemink B (2005)
Fashion in Colors: Viktor & Rolf & Kci.
New York: Editions Assouline.

Malin D (2002)
Heaven and Earth: Unseen by the Naked Eye.
London: Phaidon Press Ltd.

Martin R and Koda H (1995)
Haute Couture.
New York: The Metropolitan Museum of Art.

McDowell C (1997)
Galliano.
London: Weidenfeld & Nicolson.

McKelvey K (1996)
Fashion Source Book.
Oxford: Blackwell Publishing Ltd.

McKelvey K and Munslow J (2003)
Fashion Design: Process, Innovation and Practice.
London: Blackwell Publishing Ltd.

Nash S and Merkert J (1985)
Naum Gabo: Sixty Years of Constructivism.
Prestel-Verlag.

Newman C (2001)
National Geographic: Fashion.
Washington: National Geographic Society.

Parent M., ed. (2000)
Stella.
New York: Ipso Facto Publishers.

Powell P and Peel L (1988)
'50s & '60s Style.
London: The Apple Press Ltd.

Sorger R and Udale J (2006)
The Fundamentals of Fashion Design.
Switzerland: AVA Publishing SA.

Stipelman S (2005)
Illustrating Fashion: Concept to Creation. (2Rev Ed.)
New York: Fairchild Publications, Inc.

Research and Design

Tatham C and Seaman J (2003)
Fashion Design Drawing Course.
London: Thames & Hudson.

United Colors of Benetton (Spring/Summer 1999)
Kokeshi Dolls.

Viktor & Rolf, Premiere Decinnie (2003)
Artimo.

Wilcox C (2004)
Vivienne Westwood.
London: V&A Publications.

Wilcox C., ed. (2001)
Radical Fashion.
London: V&A Publications.

Wilcox C and Mendes V (1998)
Modern Fashion in Detail (1st Ed. 1991)
New York: The Overlook Press.

Useful resources

Research and Design

UK Contacts

British Fashion Council
5 Portland Place,
London W1B 1PW

Tel: 0207 636 7788
www.londonfashionweek.co.uk

The British Fashion Council owns and organises London Fashion Week and the British Fashion Awards. The BFC has close links with the UK's top fashion design colleges through its Colleges Forum, which acts as an interface between industry and colleges.

Skillfast-UK
Richmond House, Lawnswood
Business Park, Leeds, LS16 6RD

www.skillfast-uk.org

Skillfast-UK is the Sector Skills Council for apparel, footwear, textiles and related businesses.

The Crafts Council
44a Pentonville Road, London,
N1 9BY

Tel: 0207 278 7700
www.craftscouncil.org.uk

The Crafts Council has a contemporary gallery and crafts bookshop, as well as offering services such as advice, a reference library and development grants. It also publishes a magazine that promotes crafts.

Fashion Awareness Direct
10a Wellesley Terrace,
London, N1 7NA

Tel: 020 7490 3946
www.fad.org.uk

An organisation committed to assisting young designers succeed in fashion by bringing students and industry together at introductory events.

The London Apparel Resource Centre (ARC)

www.londonapparel.com

This centre offers designers and manufacturers the support needed to compete in today's fast moving world of fashion. Provides both training and a resource centre. Membership required.

Fashion Capital

www.fashioncapital.co.uk

Fashion Capital aims to provide a one-stop online support resource for all areas of the Clothing and Fashion industry.

Fashion United

www.fashionunited.co.uk

FashionUnited.co.uk is the business-to-business platform for the fashion industry in the UK. It offers all fashion-related websites and information, the latest fashion news and the Fashion Career Centre. The Fashion Career Centre lists current jobs in fashion, gives advice on applying and a free newsletter subscription.

US Contacts

Fashion Information
The Fashion Center Kiosk, 249
West 39th St, New York, NY 10018

Tel: +1 212 398 7943
www.fashioncenter.com

New York Fashion Council
153 East 87th Street, New York,
NY 10008
Tel: +1 212 289 0420

Pantone Color Institute

590 Commerce Boulevard,
Carlstadt, NJ 07072-3098
Tel: +1 201 935 5500
www.pantone.com

European Contacts

Modem

Modem Head Office, 30 rue de
Temple, 75004 Paris, France

Tel: +33 (0)1 48 87 08 18
Email: info@modemonline.com
www.modemonline.com

*An information resource giving an
overview of both fashion and design
from the European perspective.*

Fashion Competitions

London Graduate Fashion Week

www.gfw.org.uk

*Graduate Fashion Week was
launched in 1991 as a forum to*
*showcase the very best BA graduate
fashion design talent in the UK.*

Fashion Awareness Direct (FAD)

www.fad.org.uk

*FAD fashion competitions provide
young people with opportunities to
further their creative and practical
skills, integrate cultural research into
their work and showcase the
results to the industry and media.*

**Royal Society for the
encouragement of Arts,
Manufactures & Commerce**

www.rsadesigndirections.org

*The RSA's student annual awards
scheme, Design Directions, offers a
range of challenging projects that
comment on the changing role of
the designer in relation to society,
technology and culture.*

Can You Cut It

www.canucutit.co.uk/

*Can You Cut It, sponsored by
Skillfast-UK, the sector skills council
for apparel, textiles, footwear and*
*related businesses, features
competitions and profiles on the
'Top 10 jobs in fashion', as well as
case studies. You can also read
and listen to leading names from
the fashion world – including Lulu
Guinness and tailors from Savile
Row – give their top tips on what it
takes to succeed in what is an
extremely competitive industry.*

**Careers/ Work Experience
Contacts**

Prospects

*The Careers advice section is an
invaluable resource for graduates
looking to make the most of their
degree and develop their career.
Providing comprehensive, in-depth
career advice for graduates of any
subject, no matter what kind of
career guidance you're looking for.*

www.prospects.ac.uk

Just the Job

*A specific website that has
information on careers,
qualifications and extensive job
profiles tailored to your interests.*

www.careersinclothing.co.uk

Useful resources

Useful resources

Fabrics and Trims

UK

Cloth House
47 Berwick Street, Soho,
London, W1F 8SJ
Tel: 0207 437 5155
www.clothhouse.com

Broadwick Silks
9–11 Broadwick Street, Soho,
London, W1F 0DB
Tel: 0207 734 3320

VV Rouleaux
54 Sloane Square, Cliveden Place,
London, SW1W 8AX
Tel: 020 7730 3125
www.vvrouleaux.com

Kleins
5 Noel Street, London W1F 8GD
Tel: 0207 437 6162
www.kleins.co.uk

US

NY Elegant Fabrics, NYC
222 West 40th St., New York,
NY 10018
Tel: +11 212 302 4980
www.nyelegantfabrics.com

M&J Trimming
1008 6th Ave, New York,
NY, 10018
www.mjtrim.com

Websites

www.costumes.org

www.fashionoffice.org

www.promostyl.com

www.fashion.about.com

www.style.com

www.fashion-era.com

www.wgsn-edu.com

www.londonfashionweek.co.uk

www.premierevision.fr

www.hintmag.com

www.infomat.com

Publications and Magazines

Another Magazine	Numero Magazine
Arena Homme	Oyster
Bloom	Pop
Collezioni	Tank
Dazed and Confused	10
Drapers Record	Textile View
Elle	View on Colour
Elle Decoration	Viewpoint
ID	Viktor & Rolf
In Style	Visionaire
International Textiles	Vogue
Marie Claire	W
Marmalade	Women's Wear Daily

Fashion Forecasting

www.londonapparel.com

www.itbd.co.uk

www.modeinfo.com

www.wgsn-edu.com

www.peclersparis.com

www.edelkoort.com

Fashion Trade Shows

www.premierevision.fr

www.indigosalon.com

www.pittimmagine.com

www.purewomenswear.co.uk

www.magiconline.com

Useful resources

Courses

UK

Central Saint Martins College of Art and Design
Southampton Row, London,
WC1B 4AP
www.csm.arts.ac.uk

De Montfort University
The Gateway, Leicester, LE1 9BH
www.dmu.ac.uk

Kingston University
Knights Park, Kingston, KT1 2QJ
www.kingston.ac.uk

London College of Fashion
20 John Prince's Street, London,
W1G 0BJ
www.fashion.arts.ac.uk

Manchester Metropolitan University
All Saints Building, All Saints,
Manchester, M15 6BH
www.artdes.mmu.ac.uk/fashion/

Middlesex University Cat Hill campus
Chase Side, Barnet, Herts,
EN4 8HT
www.mdx.ac.uk

Northbrook College Sussex
Littlehampton Road, Goring-by-
Sea, West Sussex, BN12 6NU
www.northbrook.ac.uk

Northumbria University School of Design
Squires Building, Newcastle upon
Tyne, NE18ST
www.northumbria.ac.uk

Ravensbourne College of Design and Communication
Walden Road, Chislehurst, Kent,
BR7 5SN
www.rave.ac.uk

Royal College of Art
Kensington Gore, London,
SW7 2EU
www.rca.ac.uk

The Fashion Retail Academy
15–17 Gresse Street, London,
W1T 1QL
www.fashionretailacademy.ac.uk

University for the Creative Arts
(based in Canterbury, Epsom,
Farnham, Maidstone, Rochester)
www.ucreative.ac.uk

University of Brighton
Mithras House, Lewes Road,
Brighton, BN2 4AT
www.brighton.ac.uk/fashion

University of Westminster
School of Media, Arts and Design,
Watford Road, Northwick Park,
Harrow, Middlesex, HA1 3TP
www.wmin.ac.uk

Europe

Hogeschool Antwerp, Fashion Department
Nationalestraat 28/3
2000 Antwerp, Belgium
Tel. +32 3 206 08 80
Fax +32 3 206 08 82
Email : mode@ha.be

Flanders Fashion Institute
Nationalestraat 28/2
2000 Antwerp, Belgium
T: +32 3 226 14 47
FFI@modenatie.com

Parsons Paris
14 r. Letellier, 75015, Paris
www.parsons-paris.pair.com

Domus Academy
Str. 2, ed. C2 Milanofiori 20090,
Assago-Milano
www.domac.it

Amsterdam Fashion Institute
Stadhouderskade 55, 1072 AB
Amsterdam
www.amfi.hva.nl

Institucion Artistica de Ense-anza
c. Claudio Coello 48, 28001,
Madrid
www.iade.es

US

Fashion Institute of Technology
Seventh Ave. at 27, New York,
NY 10001
www.fitnyc.edu

Parsons School of Design
66 Fifth Ave., New York,
NY 10011
www.parsons.edu

Fashion Institute of Design and Merchandising
(Los Angeles, San Diego, San
Francisco, Orange County)
www.fidm.com

Research and Design

Museums and Galleries

UK

Specialist Fashion and Costume

Fashion Museum, Bath
Bennett Street, Bath, BA1 2QH
Tel: 01125 477173
www.museumofcostume.co.uk

The Victoria & Albert Museum
South Kensington, Cromwell Road,
London, SW7 2RL
Tel: 0207 942 2000
www.vam.ac.uk

Fashion and Textiles Museum
83 Bermondsey Street, London,
SE1 3XF
Tel: 0207 407 8664
www.ftmlondon.org

Museums

The British Museum
Great Russell Street, London,
WC1B 3DG
Tel: 0207 323 8000
www.thebritishmuseum.ac.uk

Natural History Museum
Cromwell Road, London, SW7 5DB
Tel: 0207 942 5000
www.nhm.ac.uk

Design Museum
Shad Thames, London, SE1 2YD
Tel: 0870 833 9955
www.designmuseum.org

Art & Craft Galleries

Tate Modern
Bankside, London, SE1 9TG
Tel: 0207 887 8888
www.tate.org.uk/modern

Barbican
The Barbican Centre, Silk Street,
London, EC2Y 8DS
Tel: 0207 638 4141
www.barbican.org.uk

Royal Academy of Arts
Burlington House, Piccadilly,
London, W1J 0BD
Tel: 0207 300 8000
www.royalacademy.org.uk

**Contemporary Applied Arts
Gallery**
2 Percy Street, London, W1
Tel: 0207 436 2344
www.caa.org.uk

The Crafts Council
44a Pentonville Road, London,
N1 9BY
Tel: 0207 278 7700
www.craftscouncil.org.uk

US

The Museum of Modern Art
11 West 53 Street, New York,
NY 10019-5497
Tel: +1 212 708 9400
www.moma.org

The Metropolitan Museum of Art
1000 Fifth Avenue at 82nd Street,
New York, NY 10028-0198
Tel: +1 212 535 7710
www.metmuseum.org

**Cooper-Hewitt, National Design
Museum**
East 91st Street, New York,
NY 10128
Tel: +1 212 849 8400
www.cooperhewitt.org

**Solomon R. Guggenheim
Museum**
1071 Fifth Avenue, New York, NY
10128-0173
Tel: +1 212 423 3500
www.guggenheim.org

**Whitney Museum of American
Art**
945 Madison Avenue at 75th
Street, New York, NY 10021
www.whitney.org

Europe

Louvre Museum
75058 Paris Cedex 01, France
www.louvre.fr

Musée d'Orsay
62, rue de Lille, 75343 Paris Cedex
07, France
www.musee-orsay.fr

**The Musée de la Mode et du
Textile**
107 rue de Rivoli, 75001 Paris,
France
www.lesartsdecoratifs.fr

**ModeMuseum Provincie
Antwerpen – MoMu**
Nationalestraat 28, 2000 Antwerp,
Belgium
www.momu.be

Triennale di Milano
Viale Alemagna, 6, 20121 Milano,
Italy
www.triennale.it

Palazzo Pitti Costume Gallery
Piazza Pitti 1, 50125 Florence, Italy
www.polomuseale.firenze.it

Japan

The Kyoto Costume Institute
103, Shichi-jo, Goshonouchi
Minamimachi, Kyoto 600–8864,
Japan
Tel: (075) 321-9219
www.kci.or.jp

Alexander McQueen

André Courrèges

Andy Warhol

Antoni Gaudi

Basso & Brooke

Christian Dior

Christian Lacroix

Christo and Jeanne-Claude

Christopher Kane

Cristobal Balenciaga

Coco Chanel

Commes des Garçons

Elsa Schiaparelli

Ernst Haeckel

Frida Kahlo

Gianni Versace

Hussein Chalayan

Issey Miyake

Jean Paul Gaultier

Jeanne Lanvin

John Galliano

Julien Macdonald

Junya Wantanabe

Manish Arora

Marc Jacobs

Mary Quant

Nicholas Ghesquiere

Oscar Wilde

Pierre Cardin

Piet Mondrian

Salvador Dali

Vivienne Westwood

Yohji Yamamoto

Yves Saint Laurent

Zora Neale Hurston

Acknowledgements and picture credits

I would like to thank everyone who has supported me during this project. In particular I would like to thank the amazing designers, Julien Macdonald, JJ at Noki, Kate Jenkins, Winni Lok at Whistles, Basso & Brooke, Bora Aksu, Manish Arora and Sarah Arnett for their creative talents and input. To David Downton, Autumn Whitehurst and Linda Ramstedt for their wonderful illustrations. Thanks to Hong Yi at Blow PR and Robert De Niet for the clothes.

A huge thank you to Rebekah Train for all her amazing design and portfolio work, and creative output for this book and its cover. To the other students, Cherri Blackwood and Lotta Lindblad, for their beautiful sketchbooks and presentation work, and to the Surface and Textiles students for their mood-boards, good luck to you in your future careers. Thanks to Catherine Redknap who assisted me in compiling all the support material at the end of this book

A special thank you goes to my dearest friend, Richard Sorger, because without his support, advice, creativity and belief in me, none of this book would have been possible. To Claire Pepper, you are an amazing photographer and without you and your talents this book would not have looked the way it does. I thank you so much for your time, creativity and patience.

Of course a huge thank you goes out to my editor, Natalia Price-Cabrera, for putting up with my mania in her office and for her support throughout, it was challenging times for us both. To Sanaz Nazemi for her amazing ability to get permission for so much for so little. To all at AVA publishing as well and to Carl and Daniel at Sifer Design for turning my endless text files and chaotic picture references into this fantastic book.

To my Mother and Father for the education they provided me with and the talents they have always encouraged. And finally to my dearest Gary who has had to put up with me and my stress for the duration of this writing process, but through it all has been wonderfully encouraging and supportive. I love you x.

Picture credits

p 3 V&A Images/Victoria and Albert Museum; p 6 Christian Dior haute couture S/S07. Designer John Galliano; p 12 NewsCast; p 18 Nigel Young/Foster + Partners; p 19 Dover Press; p 24 Sophia Kokosalaki S/S06. Catwalking.com; p 25 Ernst Haeckel. Dover Press; p 28 Givenchy haute couture A/W98. Designed by Alexander McQueen. Catwalking.com; p 28–29 Christian Lacroix: The Diary of a Collection, pp38–39. Courtesy of Thames & Hudson; p 30 Christian Dior haute couture S/S07. Designed by John Galliano. Catwalking.com; p 30 Suzuki Harunobu. Art Media/Heritage-Images; p 30 Jean Paul Gaultier S/S98. Catwalking.com; p 31 Jean Paul Gaultier. Catwalking.com; p 39 Josephine Baker (1906–75) at the Folies Bergere (b/w photo) by Walery, Stanislaus (fl.c. 1890–1920) © Private Collection/Archives Charmet/The Bridgeman Art Library. Nationality/copyright status: Polish/in copyright until 2041; pp 50–51 Dover Press; p 53 Robert Cary-Williams A/W06. Catwalking.com; p 58 Dover Press; p 64 Hussein Chalayan A/W07. Catwalking.com; p 104 Viktor & Rolf, Balls, 1998 dress, S/S98. Groninger Museum; p 107 Viktor & Rolf, Knots, 1998 dress, S/S98. Groninger Museum; p 123 Balenciaga A/W07. Designed by Nicolas Ghesquiere. Catwalking.com; p 124 Viktor & Rolf A/W03. Catwalking.com; p 125 Jonathan Saunders A/W07. Catwalking.com; p 127 Christopher Kane S/S07. Catwalking.com; p 132 V&A Images/Victoria and Albert Museum; p 132 **** Watteau pic: Photo RMN; p 134 Balenciaga prêt-à-porter S/S07. Designer Nicolas Ghesquiere. Catwalking.com; p 135 Christian Dior haute couture S/S07. Designer John Galliano; pp 152, 153 Photography Courtesy of APM; pp 5, 142 Courtesy of Autumn Whitehurst; pp 158, 159 Courtesy of David Downton; pp 66, 80 Courtesy of Julien Macdonald; pp 67, 72–73 Courtesy of Kate Jenkins, Cardigan; pp 42, 121, 138, 154 Courtesy of Linda Ramstedt; pp 67, 74–75 Courtesy of Louise Melchior for Whistles; pp 112–114 Courtesy of Sarah Arnett; pp 66, 40, 76–79, 92, 119 Richard Sorger; pp 4, 22, 23, 27, 39, 49, 54–57, 88, 90, 91 Courtesy of Simon Seivewright;pp 4, 5, 10, 15, 16, 17, 19–21, 26, 27, 32, 33, 36, 39, 40, 41, 42, 44–55, 57–63, 65–67, 70, 71–73, 76–79, 80, 82, 84–103, 107–114, 116, 118, 126, 131, 133, 136, 138, 139, 141, 145, 149, 155, 161–171, 174, 175 Photography Courtesy of Claire Pepper (www.clairepepper.co.uk); pp 4, 5, 16, 17, 40, 82, 85, 86, 88, 95, 98, 99, 107, 121, 141, 145–147, 151,155, 156 Courtesy of Rebekah Train; pp 5, 10, 19, 38, 87, 89, 100–103, 118, 120, 138, 139, 141, 144, 148, 157 Courtesy of Lotta Lindblad; pp 4, 15, 93, 149 Courtesy of Cherri Blackwood; pp 34–35 adapted from work by and Courtesy of Rhiannon Page.

Research and Design